SUCCESS

WITH

MULTICULTURAL
NEWCOMERS

&

ENGLISH LEARNERS

SUCCESS
WITH
MULTICULTURAL
& NEWCOMERS
ENGLISH LEARNERS

Proven Practices for School Leadership Teams

MARGARITA ESPINO CALDERÓN | SHAWN SLAKK

Alexandria, Virginia USA

1703 N. Beauregard St. • Alexandria, VA 22311-1714 USA
Phone: 800-933-2723 or 703-578-9600 • Fax: 703-575-5400
Website: www.ascd.org • E-mail: member@ascd.org
Author guidelines: www.ascd.org/write

Ronn Nozoe, *Interim CEO and Executive Director;* Stefani Roth, *Publisher;* Genny Ostertag, *Director, Content Acquisitions;* Susan Hills, *Acquisitions Editor;* Julie Houtz, *Director, Book Editing & Production;* Joy Scott Ressler, *Editor;* Judi Connelly, *Art Director;* Melissa Johnston, *Graphic Designer;* Keith Demmons, *Production Designer;* Mike Kalyan, *Director, Production Services;* Shajuan Martin, *E-Publishing Specialist;* Tristan Coffelt, *Production Specialist.*

PAPERBACK ISBN: 978-1-4166-1666-5   ASCD product #117026   n5/19
PDF E-BOOK ISBN: 978-1-4166-1668-9; see Books in Print for other formats.

Quantity discounts are available: e-mail programteam@ascd.org or call 800-933-2723, ext. 5773, or 703-575-5773. For desk copies, go to www.ascd.org/deskcopy.

Library of Congress Cataloging-in-Publication Data

Names: Calderón, Margarita, author. | Slakk, Shawn, author.
Title: Success with multicultural newcomers & English learners: proven
  practices for school leadership teams / Margarita Espino Calderón and
  Shawn Slakk.
Other titles: Success with multicultural newcomers and English learners
Description: Alexandria, VA USA: ASCD, [2019] | Includes bibliographical
  references and index.
Identifiers: LCCN 2018056896 (print) | LCCN 2019005736 (ebook) | ISBN
  9781416616689 (Pdf) | ISBN 9781416616665 (pbk.)
Subjects: LCSH: Immigrants--Education--United States. | Immigrant
  students--Services for--United States. | Multicultural education--United
  States. | English language--Study and teaching--Foreign speakers.
Classification: LCC LC3731 (ebook) | LCC LC3731 .C295 2019 (print) | DDC
  371.826/912--dc23
LC record available at https://lccn.loc.gov/2018056896

27 26 25 24 23 22 21 20 19   1 2 3 4 5 6 7 8 9 10 11 12

SUCCESS
WITH
MULTICULTURAL
& NEWCOMERS
ENGLISH LEARNERS

Proven Practices for School Leadership Teams

1

Identifying and Getting to Know the Newcomers and Other English Learners in Your School

Your school is experiencing a large influx of students new to the United States, and you know that more arrive in the country every day. If it hasn't already affected your school, it soon will. Schools nationwide are experiencing an increase in Newcomers and other English Learners (ELs). Are you ready for them? Most of them have limited English language skills. You and your staff wonder how best to meet their language and academic needs. Your school also has ELs who are much more advanced in their English and content learning. Should the Newcomers receive instruction in the same classrooms as the advanced ELs and the other students? Should the Newcomers have separate classroom interventions? Is a Newcomer Center needed? Does your school have enough credentialed teachers to serve the Newcomers? Are all your teachers and administrators prepared for the increase in Newcomers? What kind of professional development do you need?

We were asked to write this book as so many schools are experiencing an influx of Newcomers. As we have worked with school districts throughout the country, we've been asked the same questions: What do we do? How do we get started? How do we know if what we are doing is working?

This book is a road map for leadership teams that need to answer these questions. We hope teams of administrators, coaches, teacher leaders, and assessment specialists use our recommendations to begin to answer these questions, and those that you may have, by mapping out plans. The recommendations offered come from years of working with, listening to, and coaching administrators, coaches, and teachers from New York to Kauai. We've coached thousands of teachers in their classrooms as they implement the strategies outlined and we have combined our notes and their experiences in this book. The recommendations herein have been refined by Margarita Espino Calderón, an expert auditor for civil rights, based on her observations and documentation for various research projects, and further honed by Shawn Slakk's classroom, leadership, state agency, and professional development delivery experience. Additionally, practical ideas come from Margarita and Shawn's visits to Newcomer Centers throughout the country.

The Organization of This Book

We begin with details about a Newcomer's educational background as a foundation for expediting an individual student's learning. Getting to know the student is pivotal. With basic information in hand, the processes for formal identification, assessment, and placement in an instructional program can begin (as outlined in Chapter 2). While the academic aspects are being determined, another important learning aspect is being appraised—the socioemotional (discussed in Chapter 3). Socioemotional well-being, or lack thereof, can be the make it or break it factor in the Newcomer's productive school and life experiences.

As Newcomers and ELs are now in almost every classroom, it is incumbent on the school's entire staff to become involved in the effort to teach and care for them and to participate in professional development programs designed specifically to train staff to meet the diverse needs of Newcomers while serving all students. The research and effective practices described in Chapters 4 and 5 provide guidelines for the design of such programs. Chapters 6, 7, and 8 detail the implementation of strategies for teaching vocabulary and discourse, reading comprehension, and writing, respectively.

Professional Development Program: Key Components

The main components and purpose of the professional development program aimed at training staff to meet the needs of Newcomer and ELs (as illustrated in Figure 1.1) are:

- Identifying your students
- Identifying your qualified teachers and staff
- Developing a programmatic structure of service

- Accelerating ELs' language, literacy, and knowledge base
- Supporting Newcomers' socioemotional well-being
- Designing, implementing, and sustaining professional development for all staff

FIGURE 1.1 Key Components of Professional Development Program

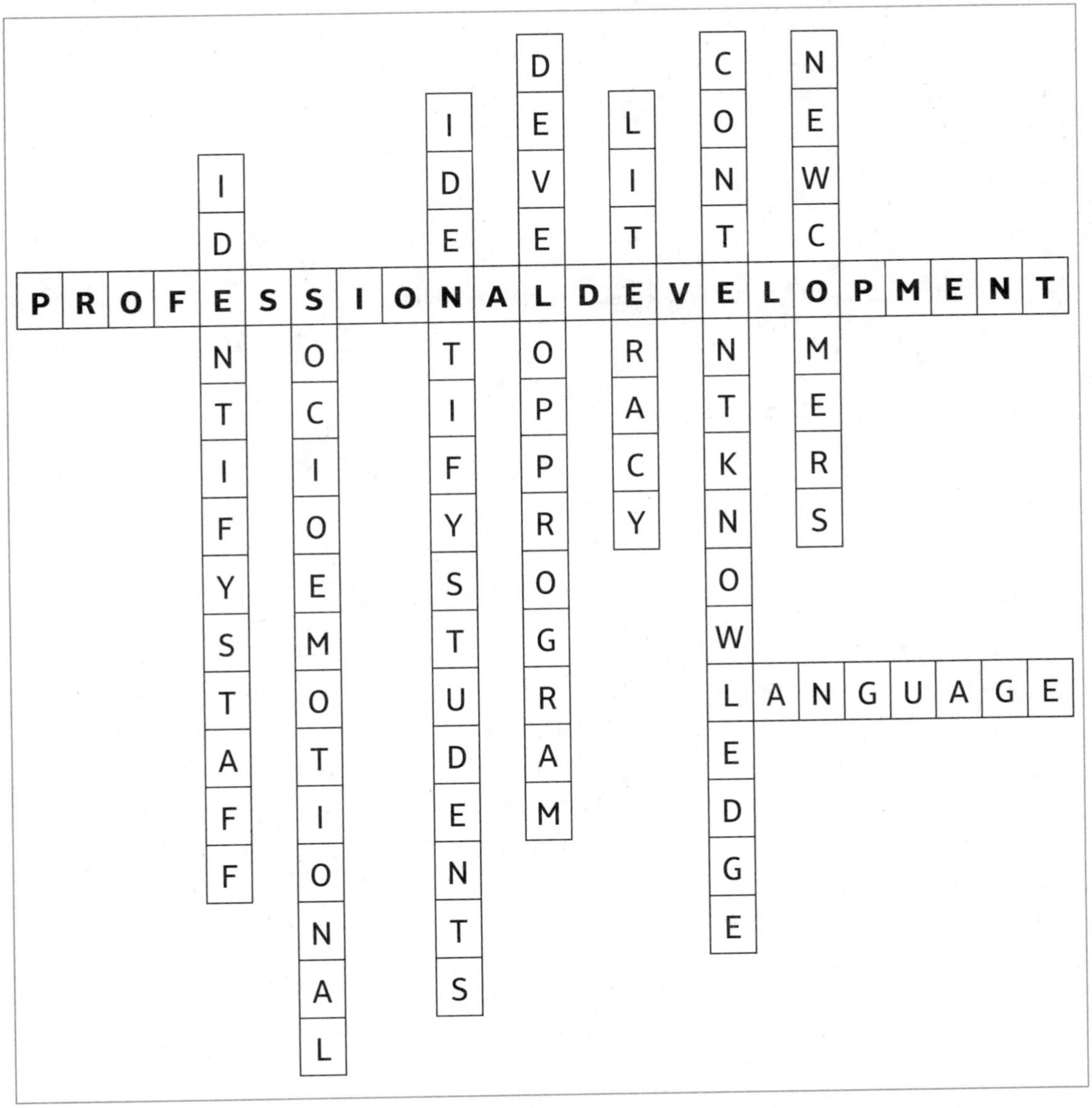

We will address each of these items to help you develop your plan. If you already have a plan or a program, when you meet in collegial teams, you can review to identify gaps, progresses, and successes.

We offer evidence-based, effective instructional practices in Chapters 6, 7, and 8.

> For years, it was thought that Newcomers had to wait to start reading and writing. It is our contention that this myth has delayed students and is the primary reason why there are so many long-term ELs. Our research and practice indicate that with certain systematic instructional strategies, coupled with socioemotional approaches, Newcomers can excel.

Who Are Your Newcomers?

Do you know who your Newcomers are and where they come from? Culturally responsive teaching begins by knowing your students' histories, cultures, experiences, and canons. The more we know about each student, the better we can build on their strengths and scaffold success in rigorous core-content curricula (LeMoine & Soto, 2017). After you discuss the following with your registrar or intake center personnel, you can use the chart shown in Figure 1.2 to map out the educational experiences and needs of your Newcomers.

Classification of Newcomers and Other ELs

- *Refugees.* These students are from places made inhospitable by severe violence and war. Refugee parents can apply for U.S. permanent resident status after one year from legal entry and then may request U.S. citizenship after five years. When refugees arrive, they are placed near private resettlement agencies that assist them with housing and job placement.
- *Non-Refugee Newcomers.* These are students from, for example, Mexico, India, China, and Cuba, as well as well as students displaced by natural disasters (who are ineligible for refugee status). They may not possess the U.S. residency permits necessary for them to receive governmental aid.

FIGURE 1.2 2nd to 12th Grade Newcomers: Language and Literacy in First Languages Continuum

←—No Schooling in First Language (L1)————————————————————————————Literate in L1—→

Students with Limited or Interrupted Formal Education				Highly Schooled EL
Unschooled SLIFE	**SIFE**	**Schooled SLIFE**		
No schooling	Missing 2+ years of elementary or secondary level	Missing 1–2 years of elementary level	Missing 1–2 years of secondary level	Significant schooling
New to print	Some L1 literacy	Elementary level L1 literacy	Some L1 reading skills but limited writing	Grade level L1 reading and writing skills
Need alphabet, phonics, sound to letter concepts, concept of word, basal beginning word/vocabulary study, reading and orthographic/writing skills	Need advanced phonics, long/short vowels, syllables and affixes, concept of words in text, grammar and mechanics, vocabulary, basic reading and writing	Need elementary word/vocabulary study, reading comprehension skills, and text-based writing	Need secondary advanced content words, more vocabulary study, multiple genre reading comprehension skills, and text-based writing	Need vocabulary labels for known concepts, reading comprehension, and text-based writing skills
Need language for socioemotional expression and survival in school and community	Need language for socioemotional expression and survival in school and community	Need language for socioemotional expression and survival in school and community	Need language for socioemotional expression and survival in school and community	Need language for socioemotional expression and survival in school and community

NOTE

Students from Puerto Rico, though U.S. citizens, are sometimes classified as non-refugee Newcomers as, due to their educational system's "Spanish as the official language" policy and newness to English, their English proficiency is limited.

- *Highly Schooled Newcomers (HSN).* These students are children of government officials, professionals, and other highly schooled immigrants from all over the world, with the highest numbers from India. These students may speak great English but may need cultural and pronunciation assistance. Even those from countries where English is a national language—Liberia, South Africa, Singapore—might have gaps in dialect, reading comprehension skills that meet state standards, and cultural adaptation.

- *Students with Limited or Interrupted Formal Education (SLIFE)/Students with Interrupted Formal Education (SIFE).* These students arrive in 2nd to 12th grades with little or no education experiences in their previous countries (see Figure 1.2 for more details). Their language, literacy, and content knowledge may also be limited in their primary languages. Hence, they may need basic decoding skills and emergent writing skills, along with abundant vocabulary.
- *Dually Identified Newcomers.* These students also need to be considered for special education services. They must be assessed 30 days after arriving, per the Every Student Succeeds Act guidelines, and receive both English as a Second Language/ English Language Development (ESL/ELD) and special education services.

Other EL Students New to Your School

The following ELs not new to the United States, who have more advanced English skills, may also arrive at your school:

- *Migrant ELs.* These are students who are most likely born here and thus could fit in several categories of ELs or non-ELs. Migrant students travel with their parents from state to state following the crops or other temporary job opportunities. State Migrant Education offices typically have records of their schooling from the various places in which they have resided.
- *Long-Term ELs (LTELs).* These are students who are most likely U.S. citizens, perhaps second- or third-generation, and have had U.S. EL status for at least five years. They, unfortunately, did not receive quality instruction. The U.S. Department of Education publications state that 70 percent or more of all students categorized as ELs are LTELs.
- *Dreamers.* These are undocumented students who were brought here by their parents. They constantly fear deportation. They often work and study relentlessly and are on track to attend college.
- *Standard English Learners (SELs).* California uses this term for students who were never classified as ELs but who speak nonstandard forms of English (e.g., Chicano English or African American vernacular English) and have academic linguistic needs. The dialects and language that they bring to school should be built upon and not viewed as a deficit (Soto-Hinman & Hertzel, 2009).

Some of these categories overlap. Migrant ELs could be SLIFE or SIFE. A Dreamer could be an SEL who is proficient and excelling in English. Some Migrant ELs may be SIFE and others valedictorians. Unfortunately, despite the wide range of background knowledge and skills, we have observed in many schools that Newcomers are typically grouped together with LTELs in the same ESL/ELD classrooms. This makes it very difficult for ESL/ELD teachers to reach students at diverse levels. The usual solution is to teach to the middle. The usual isn't working for many of these students, nor is giving ESL/ELD teachers only 25 to 30 minutes to try to address this variety of language and cultural needs!

Figure 1.2 highlights characteristics of background schooling experiences that intake assessment personnel can identify and share with the school's teachers and support personnel. With this information, the leadership team can begin to map out program designs and staffing configurations. Knowing the amount of schooling in the primary language will help the team determine how quickly a student might progress to standard academic achievement and who will need additional support.

Identifying Newcomers' Schooling Experiences

Newcomers' instructional needs vary considerably, even within the realm of vocabulary and oracy. Due to this diversity, Newcomers should not be grouped together arbitrarily. Figure 1.2 outlines some of the ways they can be grouped based on main differences in their first language literacy skills.

Taking into account the early childhood education of the students' guardians is also helpful in placing the students in programs suited to their learning progressions (see Figure 1.3). All parents want their children to succeed—which is usually a big part of why they come to this country. Regardless of their education levels and/or dominant languages, they often have two or three jobs to make ends meet. Even highly educated parents who have diplomatic jobs or similar responsibilities are affected by time constraints. This means that they may not have quality time to read to their children or attend school events and meetings. It is not that they don't care. It is out of necessity as they work hard to build better futures for their children. More importantly, they have complete confidence that their children's teachers will take care of their children's education. Many come from cultures that fully entrust their children's education to you, the teacher.

Newcomers and Long-Term ELs: Similar but Different

It is critically important to differentiate Newcomers from the LTELs—although on the surface some may appear to have the same needs. While LTELs sound more fluent in their everyday discourse as well as when they read, when asked what they read,

FIGURE 1.3 Preschool to 1st Grade Newcomers and Their Parents: Language Learning Continuum

←————No School in First Language (L1) or English————————Highly Schooled in L1 and English————→

Years of Language Learning in School				Highly Schooled
Unschooled	**Limited Start**	**Limited Schooling**		
Parents had no or limited schooling in L1 and none in English; child had no schooling in either language.	Parents had limited schooling in L1 and none in English; child had no preschool in either language.	Parents had elementary and secondary schooling in L1 but no schooling in English; child had no preschool or kindergarten in either language.	Parents had elementary and secondary schooling in L1 and some schooling in English; child had preschool and kindergarten in L1 and some exposure to English.	Parents are college educated in L1 and English as a second language or received higher education in English; child had preschool and kindergarten in L1 and possibly English as a second language or English as a foreign language

they may not be able to tell you (as their comprehension is limited). As stated previously, LTELs are often second- or third-generation U.S. citizens and have been taught in U.S. schools since kindergarten or for at least five years. They have received inadequate education in English academic language and literacy. Approximately 70 to 80 percent of ELs in most school districts are LTELs. Figure 1.4 outlines some of the needs and characteristics of LTELs to help you distinguish them.

What to Consider Before Assessing and Planning

Federal and state guidelines expect you to identify ELs as quickly as possible when they arrive at your school. At the beginning of the year, schools have 30 days to identify students whose primary language is not English and assess these students' ELD levels to determine who may need additional English language learning support. Therefore, we recommend starting the processes and conversations needed to assess and learn who your Newcomers are now, before they arrive. This chapter provides guidelines to identify the subcategories of Newcomers, but the process does not stop there. To properly serve these students, all educators in your school need to find out as much as necessary about the students

FIGURE 1.4 **4th to 12th Grade Long-Term ELs: Literacy in First Languages and in English Continuum**

←———————————— Years in U.S. Schools ————————————→

Most elementary schooling in L1 and some ESL in bilingual programs	Most L1 instruction in bilingual programs and some general education with push-in ESL	Interrupted formal education due to migrant life or trips to native country	English-only instruction but unable to pass reclassification test or state exams	Passed reclassification test but struggling to pass state tests
Needs: vocabulary, intensive phonics, writing development	Needs: vocabulary for basic reading comprehension and writing skills	Needs: ample vocabulary and assessments to determine which reading and writing skills can be enhanced	Needs: extensive vocabulary and assessments to determine which reading and writing skills can be enhanced	Needs: extensive vocabulary and assessments to determine which reading and writing skills can be enhanced

All Long-Term ELs need self-efficacy skills, a mindset for success in school and career planning, and relationship building. Some students who were reclassified two or more years earlier may still fall within this category. Now that ESSA calls for four years of monitoring after reclassification, these skills should be considered as ongoing until graduation. Even third- and fourth-generation Hispanic students who are Standard English Learners might benefit from socioemotional skills and career planning.

and their family backgrounds—enough to provide the correct program of service without being invasive.

Identification and placement in the appropriate program of service starts on day one. ELs who arrive during the school year must be identified and screened within 14 school days of enrollment (U.S. Department of Justice & U.S. Department of Education, 2015). For this reason, the Office for Civil Rights at the U.S. Department of Education and the Civil Rights Division at the U.S. Department of Justice recommend that every Local Education Agency and school district have a process in place to identify ELs upon arrival. This initial screening typically takes the form of a Home Language Survey. Each school should know and implement their district's process.

Home Language Survey

Your school can administer the Home Language Survey (HLS) to parents as part of the initial enrollment and registration process, especially at the New Student Welcome

Center if there is one, to identify students whose native language is not English. It does not need to be long or invasive. The following four questions work well:

1. What language do you speak with your child at home?
2. What language does your child speak at home with you?
3. What language does your child speak with friends?
4. What language did your child speak when learning how to talk?

An additional step is to have the HLS, the identification process, and the explanation of how it all aids the student translated into other languages. Some schools and district offices have translators or a call-in service that can provide the explanations in several languages to help parents with the survey. This extra step will help parents understand the need for ESL services and why the HLS questions are asked.

Frequently, parents do not understand the questions (since they are written in English) or do not want it known that their children speak another language. If your school has a bilingual program, parents are often reluctant to have their child participate, because they believe there is too much primary language and not enough English. Beyond the letter of the law, having a printed translation or a person to assist with registration makes the process easier, more accurate, and less uncomfortable for all.

If a parent answers any of the HLS questions in a language other than English, the school or district is required to screen this student for his or her ELD level and communicate the results to the student's parents along with the intended scope of service.

At this stage, parent communication is crucial. Parents and students need to be assured that their private information will remain private. In addition, attention should be placed on the purpose and importance of this process. Many parents may be leery of providing this information or have heard misinformation about this process. Interpreters should be provided for those whom the school staff cannot assist. Provide detailed explanations and assurances as to why this process is happening, how the possible services benefit the students for their academic success, and that it is their right to expect this assistance. Every effort should be taken to accurately obtain the answers to HLS's four simple questions. It is both an expectation of federal and state guidelines and an ethical responsibility to ensure the success of the students, the teachers, and the school.

English Language Development Screening

After you administer the HLS and identify incoming ELs, you need to continue the screening process with an English language placement test. You must assess these students' needs, set a plan for their specific educational programs, and implement a process for monitoring and assessing their progress over time—including beyond the point when they meet the exit criteria. The ESSA requires four years of monitoring for students who have exited EL status to ensure continued progress and success.

While each district may choose its own screening instrument, the screening instrument must evaluate a student's English language levels at grade level as well as evaluate the student's proficiency with the components of English language usage and grammar in the four language domains—reading, writing, listening, and speaking. If the results of the ELD-level screener indicate that the student is not an EL, the process ends, and the student should be scheduled as any other student.

We have been in schools where a second look into the students' records helped to see what, if any, services they have received. Although typical for most ELs, it is unlikely for Newcomers to have such records. Therefore, in these schools, Newcomers' records are started right away. They are also double-checked twice per year to ensure compliance, proper service, and avoidance of redundancy.

In some instances, the general classroom teacher is the best source to verify a student's needs.

> At one school, Shawn realized that at registration, the parents of Boris, a 2nd grader whose home language was Russian, filled in "English" in response to all the HLS questions. As a result, Boris had not been screened for his ELD level. After a brief investigation and a conversation with Boris's parents, Shawn learned that an adult relative serving as a translator for the parents had completed the forms. Boris's parents, who did not fully understand the process or the reason behind the questionnaire, had been incorrectly informed that if they responded with any language other than English, their son would be sent to a school outside of the neighborhood and would not receive instruction in English. Unfortunately, Shawn did not find this out until more than a year after Boris was in class and failing to thrive. It was only as a last act of desperation by Boris's teacher that Shawn was asked to help. Boris wasn't on the rosters as being a Limited English Proficiency (LEP) student, and Shawn arrived at the school after Boris, so he was unaware of the services that Boris needed. Fortunately, after a conference (facilitated by a Russian interpreter) with Boris, his parents, and his teacher, Boris was correctly identified as an EL and immediately began receiving services—and has now successfully exited EL status and is headed to high school.

Getting Started

To start planning and assessing your school's program of service to ELs, you will need to determine (1) what you need to address in your plan, (2) what you currently have in place, and (3) what you have that has proved effective for EL success.

We introduced the rubric presented in Figure 1.5 to a middle school in Virginia at the beginning of training. The leadership team, ESL teachers, and content area chairs wanted to know where they stood with identification of EL students, tracking progress, and their own professional development. They reviewed this plan every quarter to gauge progress on each item. You also can use this tool to begin your journey.

FIGURE 1.5 **Rubric for EL Services Assessment and Analysis**

Process Component	Needed (planning notes)	Started (what else we need)	Successful (what we're looking for as proof)
How do we identify and assess Newcomers?	*No current plan. These students are sent to us from the district office.*	*Need to train intake staff on processes and policies to verify students are correctly identified.*	*Use our HLS during registration process.* *Staff identifies misidentified students and corrects problems.*
How do we develop and use an HLS and communicate with parents about it?	*We use the HLS provided by the district.*	*We wrote explanations and translations but need interpretation services to help parents and registrar.*	*All intake staff are aware of policy, process, and resources for communicating with parents during registration.*
How do we identify highly qualified teachers and staff for Newcomers?	*Review state and federal guidelines for adequate service.*	*Registrar is aware of teachers who are trained in ExC-ELL and places Newcomers in those classes where possible.*	*All teachers are trained in ExC-ELL.*
What is the programmatic structure of service?	*This is under review.*	*District provides service parameters, but we need to review our specific population's needs.*	*All EL service hours and requirements meet or exceed federal and/or district guidelines.* *Students make adequate yearly progress and exit ESL services.*

Process Component	Needed (planning notes)	Started (what else we need)	Successful (what we're looking for as proof)
How are we accelerating Newcomer language, literacy, and knowledge base?	*Produce a road map after completing our professional development on evidence-based instruction.*	*We need to develop a Newcomer EL TLC and instructional team.*	*Students are making adequate yearly progress and exiting from ESL services.*
How are we addressing Newcomer socioemotional well-being?	*This is under review.*	*Counselors have received PD but need to redeliver this PD to all staff.*	*Anecdotal evidence.*
What EL-targeted professional development do we provide for all staff?	*Whole-school PD on Newcomer strategies. Content teachers with one or more Newcomers need immediate PD on assessing content and language needs and providing appropriate instruction.*	*ESL/ELD teachers need PD on current practices for teaching the four domains. ESL and core-content teachers need PD on co-teaching.*	*All staff are trained, coached, and regularly observed implementing ExC-ELL strategies in all content and lessons.*

Fill in as much as possible of this rubric as a team and review your identified needs assessment. Your next step is student assessment and placement. Your program planning process will stay fluid as your team continues to explore the status of each question, visiting and revisiting the identification, assessment, and placement process. Revisiting the federal guidelines for this initial process will remind and inform everyone in the school of the requirements. Requirements and recommendations are detailed in Chapter 2.

Summary

Getting to know Newcomers at a deeper level benefits them, the teachers, and the whole school. Connecting with their parents throughout this journey builds the trust and confidence necessary for continuous, positive relationships. Although you may already have a program for ELs in place, revisit the federal guidelines, current research, and the manner in which other schools are moving forward and integrating ESL/ELD and Newcomer Centers with general education teachers and staff. As well, an annual review is a good way to ensure that the ever-changing needs of students are being met. Sharing with the whole school critical data on the status of your plan helps make it a team effort. The ESL/ELD teachers can no longer be the sole staff members who address the needs of Newcomers/ELs. The whole school must be involved.

2 Assessing Your Students' Academic Needs

You and your colleagues have just spent several days working on and planning how to correctly screen, identify, and welcome Newcomers and the other ELs who have recently moved to your community. The training and discussion revolved around the changes by ESSA to the Elementary and Secondary Education Act. As your school receives Title I funding, these changes require your school and district, as guided by your state educational agency, to create and implement standardized entrance and exit procedures for ELs. The opening of school is quickly approaching, and your team has realized that the new changes require them to assess all students who may be ELs within 30 days of enrollment at your school [ESEA section 3113(b)(2)].

As outlined in Chapter 1, identifying ELs is a federal requirement; it is also crucial for the ELs and their teachers. Identification of ELs in a timely manner—within 30 days at the beginning of the year and within 14 days during the school year —is also a federal requirement, and beneficial for all. Effective instruction needs to begin the moment ELs enter the classrooms, and personalized plans for this instruction need to be based on proper, prior assessment of each EL's instructional needs, ESL/ELD level, and the EL program implemented by the school.

Initial Process and Assessment for Placement in Programs

There are two phases of assessment. The first phase is to determine students' educational backgrounds, including identifying background knowledge of English and subject matter, upon entry to the school system. The second phase is to assess their learning progressions in the four language domains—listening, speaking, reading, and writing—in the content areas of math, science, language arts, and social studies.

This chapter lays out the process and assessments for identifying background knowledge of English and subject matter and placing the student in an appropriate program of instruction. It hinges on guidelines set forth by the U.S. Department of Justice (USDOJ) and the U.S. Department of Education (USDOE): informing parents, using appropriate placement assessments, and the types of programs into which to place the student that would meet compliance. Ongoing performance assessments to be used throughout the year are outlined in Chapters 6 (Vocabulary and Discourse), 7 (Teaching Reading Comprehension), and 8 (Teaching Writing).

Informing Parents and Students Is a Priority!

Once a student is identified as an EL, the student's parents must be notified that their child qualifies for English language assistance (USDOJ & USDOE, 2015). In addition to the notification of services, parents need to be properly informed of

- Their rights
- The extent of or reason for additional services
- Their child's ESL/ELD level and how it was determined
- The programmatic and instructional services that their child will receive
- How services will interweave (e.g., ESL with counseling and special education)
- EL exit criteria

Parents have the option to decline (waive or opt out of) direct services. However, their children would still be identified as ELs, need to be monitored, tested annually, and served in general education classrooms until they have exited EL status.

Waiving or Opting Out of Services

Parents "waiving" or "opting out" of services does not abrogate the obligation of the Local Educational Agency (LEA) or the school to provide a student with EL support.

This federal mandate needs to be conveyed to the parents and the student. Diligence is required to help parents and students understand that waiving or opting out of direct services does not release the LEA/school district from continuing to document the student's ESL/ELD level and progress and performing an annual assessment until such time as the student exits EL status. On the contrary, clear communication with parents and students as to the benefits of having ESL support and services is an ethical duty. The teacher, counselor, or administrator whose responsibility it is to ensure proper identification and assurance of services will need to be insistent in explaining the academic benefits of ESL services and support (such as a bilingual program) as well as the deleterious possibilities of not receiving direct services—students may be less successful or even fail and have to retake courses if they are not afforded the proper support and assistance with learning English and have no recourse for future assistance.

Why do some parents waive services? We have found that parents are sometimes misinformed about the service delivery process or what services entail. The parents may have had bad experiences in the past with other schools or never received an explanation of the benefits of ESL services for their children.

> In one instance, the written Chinese version of the explanation of services was incorrect, leading parents to believe that the school wanted to provide special education services for their child's learning disability—a disability the parents knew the student didn't have. This became the urban myth of the community, and members of the Chinese community of the school always opted out. Others thought that their students would not be able to participate in after-school sports activities or in orchestra were they to be identified as ELs. Fortunately, both situations were resolved after a review of the translated document, the process, and some communication with the parents and community.

Communication of Federal Guidelines

A first step is to inform faculty, administrators, counselors, and office staff that the waiving or opting out of EL programs by the parents of an EL does not absolve parents or teachers of monitoring and providing support and assistance to ELs, and that all parties will be increasingly scrutinized by supervising agencies (such as the USDOJ and the USDOE-Office of Civil Rights [OCR]).

During a USDOE-OCR or USDOJ review, it would be standard protocol for the USDOJ attorneys or reviewers to visit the school, as they have done and continue to do in many states in large and small school districts. You will be expected to have Newcomer/EL records with all the information listed in Chapters 1 and 2.

Documentation

In addition to identifying a student as knowing, speaking, using, or hearing a language other than English in the home, the federal guidelines also call for documenting Newcomers who may have other needs based upon their background, home and schooling experiences, and where they come from. This requires that the school have adequate translation and assistance resources available to accomplish this screening, as well as proper training for those who will alert staff of students who show signs of distress or who may need other socioemotional or physiological services. A district or school that does not properly screen incoming students is also out of compliance with the Every Student Succeeds Act (ESSA).

In Chapter 4, we will look more closely at the staffing and professional development needs that must be considered when a school or district is screening Newcomers and designing programs for them. Chapter 3 focuses on addressing socioemotional needs and other noncurricular issues that impact student academic success as much as quality instruction.

Language Assistance Programs

Schools can choose from among several program options for their Newcomers. When implemented, a language assistance program (LAP), or services, must be educationally sound in theory and effective in practice. However, the civil rights laws of the United States do not require any particular program or method of instruction for ELs (USDOJ & USDOE, 2015). The important caveat is that students in EL programs must receive appropriate language assistance services until they are proficient in English and can participate meaningfully in the district's educational programs without language assistance (USDOJ & USDOE, 2015). This has implications for finding the most effective and efficient program that will put ELs on a smooth and timely path to academic achievement and will help the school maintain exemplary status.

The following are the programs that USDOJ and USDOE recommend (noting both that for language services, we are quoting their descriptions below since detail and language is extremely important and that each regulation and options is followed by notes from us based on common trends in schools across the country):

- *English as a Second Language (ESL).* Also known as English Language Development (ELD), this is a program of techniques, methodology, and special curriculum designed explicitly to teach ELs about the English language, including the academic vocabulary needed to access content instruction, and to develop their English language proficiency in the four language domains—listening, speaking, reading, and writing. ESL instruction is usually in English with little use of the ELs' primary languages (USDOJ & USDOE, 2015). It was previously thought that ELs needed to develop listening and then speaking before they could learn to read and write in English. ELs would go from year to year receiving special listening and speaking instructions in their pull-out ESL classes, because it was erroneously thought that they couldn't handle learning core subjects. Newer studies conclude that listening and speaking develop faster and at higher levels when integrated with reading and writing (August & Shanahan, 2008; Calderón, 2007; National Academies of Science, Engineering, and Medicine, 2017). It is our contention, based on these studies, that this delay is the reason why there are so many LTELs throughout the country.

NOTE

ESL/ELD instruction is usually delivered in "pull-out" programs, where a credentialed teacher pulls ELs from their core classrooms for 30 to 45 minutes per day. Another option is for the ESL/ELD teacher to "push into" a core classroom and co-teach with the core-content teacher. When the ESL/ELD teacher comes into a class and goes from EL to EL to translate or assist, this does not count toward the time on ESL learning. It usually means spending only 3 or so minutes per student instead of the 30 to 45 minutes required.

- *Structured English Immersion (SEI).* This is a program designed to impart English language skills so that the EL, when proficient in English, can transition and succeed in an English-only mainstream classroom. All instruction in an immersion strategy program is delivered in English. Teachers have specialized training in meeting the needs of ELs (e.g., an ESL teaching credential and/or SEI training) and have demonstrated strong skills in promoting ELD and SEI strategies to ensure EL students' access to content (USDOJ & USDOE, 2015).

NOTE

Some states—including Florida, Nevada, and Massachusetts (and California until 2017, when new legislation passed permitting dual-language programs again)—have English-only or SEI programs. ESL/ELD requirements are also part of these program requirements. The Massachusetts instructional program was developed following the ExC-ELL instructional model that we will describe in Chapters 6, 7, and 8.

- *Transitional Bilingual Education (TBE).* Also known as early-exit bilingual education, this is a program that utilizes a student's primary language in instruction. The program maintains and develops skills in the primary language while introducing, maintaining, and developing skills in English. The primary purpose of a TBE program is to facilitate the EL student's transition to an all-English instructional program, while the student receives academic subject instruction in the primary language to the extent necessary (USDOJ & USDOE, 2015).

NOTE

The USDOJ also recommends planning for 80 percent of core instruction in the primary language and two periods of ESL/ELD for Newcomers. As ELs learn more English, they can begin to take core content in English, usually math or other SEI content, along with one ESL/ELD class. One caveat is to avoid keeping Newcomers in their primary language longer than two or three years. The instructional program BCIRC (See Calderón, Hertz-Lazarowitz, & Slavin, 1998 or BCIRC in the What Works Clearinghouse) enabled students to pass their state exit exams in two or three years (after which time they are in danger of becoming LTELs).

- *Dual-Language Program.* Also known as two-way, developmental, or 50-50, this is a bilingual program where the goal is for students to develop language proficiency in two languages by receiving instruction in English and another language in a classroom that usually comprises half primary-English speakers and half primary of the other language (USDOJ & USDOE, 2015).

NOTE

This is one of the most difficult programs to implement or make successful. When educators feel uncertain about total immersion in two languages, they begin to tweak, modify, then change the program into something unidentifiable. The result is that students stop making adequate progress in these loose couplings and dual-language programs are deemed unsuccessful.

In school districts or schools where the number of ELs is small, ELs still must receive language assistance services; however, the EL program may be less formal (USDOJ & USDOE, 2015).

NOTE

When small numbers of ELs are distributed throughout the school, we recommend that all staff be trained to work with ELs—who will continually arrive.

Meeting Compliance

Examples of when the USDOJ and the USDOE (2015) have identified compliance issues include when school districts:

- Exclude kindergarteners, or ELs with scheduling conflicts, from EL programs.
- Supplement regular education instruction with only aides who tutor EL students as opposed to teachers adequately trained to deliver the EL program.
- Fail to offer an EL program to a certain subset of EL students, such as students with disabilities or students speaking particular languages.
- Stop providing language assistance services when EL students reach higher levels of English proficiency but have not yet met exit criteria (including proficiency on a valid and reliable ELP assessment).
- Fail to address the needs of EL students who have not made expected progress in learning English and have not met exit criteria despite extended enrollment in the EL program.

We urge your school to spend quality time designing and using these criteria for evaluating your program continuously. As Expert Consultant, USDOJ, Margarita has spent eight years making recommendations to schools through the DOJ for attaining and sustaining compliance. It all comes down to revisiting this chapter to make sure your school is in compliance with the USDOJ and USDOE requirements.

Newcomer Centers

Any of the aforementioned programs, and their requirements, can be implemented in Newcomer Centers. A Newcomer Center can be a school within a school or a separate school, depending on the number of students. One important point to remember is that students cannot be isolated from general education peers. This means that after ESL/ELD with SEI or bilingual instruction, the rest of the day should be spent in core-content classrooms. Some Newcomer Centers bus their Newcomers to the closest school for half a day. Others have ESL/ELD-certified core-content teachers who teach math, science, or social studies.

Providing Equity in an EL Program

In addition to providing English language assistance, the USDOJ requires that ELs/Newcomers have equitable grade-level content, enabling them to meet college and career readiness standards. Districts are obligated to ensure that all ELs have an equal opportunity to participate in all programs—academic or otherwise—including but not limited to prekindergarten, magnet, gifted and talented, career and technical education, arts, and athletics programs; advanced placement courses, STEM/STEAM; clubs; and honors societies (USDOE, 2016).

Instruction and programming for ELs/Newcomers must reach the students where they are and build their language and literacy through content. This instruction must include all programs a school offers, supplemental or not. In Chapter 5, we will see how professional development must and can be provided across the school, so that appropriate language support can be supplied in all subject areas. The whole-school approach integrates ESL/ELD instruction with general education. It can be called a dual-language, bilingual, ESL/ELD, sheltered-instruction, or structured-immersion program. What is different is that all teachers in the school receive the same professional development on working with Newcomers/ELs. They continue to meet in learning communities to sustain their own learning and program implementation as well as gauge the students' learning progressions. Chapter 4 describes the whole-school approach further and gives examples of how exemplary schools implement the models.

Summary

The Newcomer identification process includes:

1. Identifying Newcomers with a Home Language Survey followed by an appropriate assessment of their listening, speaking, reading, and writing levels in English.
2. Informing Newcomers' parents of the results of Newcomers' screenings and assessments, placement in a particular program for English language development, the school's obligation, parents' rights to waive/opt out of a program, and the legal service requirements with or without direct service.
3. Ensuring that the Newcomer has equal opportunities for participating in curricular and extracurricular activities and programs (which will be covered in subsequent chapters).
4. Ensuring that every staff member, teacher, and other administrators in your school receive appropriate training to understand, communicate, instruct, and support the Newcomers and their parents.

To help you plan and assess your school's intake, identification, and communication process, the rubric presented in Figure 2.1 can get you started.

> We have been working with a large urban school with a history of working with Newcomers. In a relatively short period of time, the school's Newcomer population increased from 10 to 42—and more were on the way. The administration realized that one ESL/ELD teacher could no longer singlehandedly be responsible for instructing the growing Newcomer population. As they began their discussions, the administration realized that their old plan for properly identifying their Newcomers and placing them in quality programs needed revamping. As they were planning the program for Newcomers, they realized that the core-content teachers who would come in contact with Newcomers needed extensive training. The ESL teachers also felt that their training had been "somewhat archaic" and wanted to learn better ways of reaching their students. At the end of their second meeting, we collected their initial self-assessment and filled in the rubric (see Figure 2.1) as an example of what they felt they needed, what had been started and needed further development, and what processes they felt they felt had been successfully implemented.

FIGURE 2.1 Rubric for the Identification of ELs

Process Component	Needed (planning notes)	Started (what else we need)	Successful (what we're looking for as proof)
Assessment and evaluation of ESL/ELD levels	*Team needs to evaluate our processes this summer to plan next year's professional development (PD) and improvement plans.*	*District uses the W-APT, but our staff needs further PD on what the cores and assessment means for instruction.*	*All teachers are aware of WIDA and what ACCESS 2.0 test scores mean for their students and how to implement effective strategies for growth in lessons. Leadership teams see evidence of ESL/ELD strategies in lessons.*
Parent communication • Child's EL status • ESL/ELD service benefits and requirements • Parents' rights • School's obligations	*Team needs to evaluate our processes this summer to plan next year's PD and improvement plans.* *Need to evaluate who in the community can help and what district resources we have.*	*We have written explanations and translations but need to find interpretation services to help parents, counselors, and teachers with conferences and questions.*	*All parents who enter the school are easily able to get assistance in their primary language.*
ESL/ELD program options	*We can choose a dual-language model or ESL/ELD (more time for Levels 1 and 2) coupled with trained core-content teachers with whom ELs spend the rest of the day.*	*Need to evaluate program implementation and EL success.* *Need to plan next year's whole-school implementation.*	*ACCESS 2.0 and year-end tests show EL growth.* *Percentage of students exiting ESL status is increasing.*
Equitable EL participation in curriculum, activities, programs, and services	*Scheduling team and ESL teachers need to collaborate on allowing EL time for ESL services, electives, and advanced placement courses.*	*We need to review the schedule, check for equity, and adjust as needed.*	*Documentation and general observation show all students have equitable access to all activities, programs, and services.*
Staff training to support, understand, and communicate about correct EL identification and service	*We need to evaluate our processes.*	*ESL teachers trained on these processes.* *All staff needs to be informed and aware of their obligations.*	*Documentation and program reviews show all students are properly served and identified.*

3 Understanding Your Students' Social and Emotional Needs

Social and emotional learning is the process through which children and adults acquire and effectively apply the knowledge, attitudes, and skills necessary to understand and manage emotions, set and achieve positive goals, feel and show empathy for others, establish and maintain positive relationships, and make responsible decisions (CASEL, 2019).

As detailed in Chapter 1, Newcomers come with a diversity of skills, talents, experiences, and needs. These awesome English learners may have faced myriad difficult situations coming to this country and upon arrival. Some come at a young age, while others as adolescents. Many come with families, extended families, or no families (as in the case of unaccompanied minors). Many ELs, especially Newcomers, experience numerous degrees of challenges, such as moving to a new country, trying to fit into a new school and adapting to a different type of learning, a different school culture, and different expectations, significantly different from where they went to school before, if they were able to attend school at all. Add in tackling the arduous task of learning a different language while learning math, science, social studies, and language arts. Even something as simple as arriving at school on time every day may be a different concept to learn. This new learning curve also applies to the Newcomers' parents as they, too, will be getting used to a new culture, process, and set of expectations while dealing with the other aspects of moving and living in a new country.

Enlisting the Whole School and Community

The research is conclusive: explicit instruction of socioemotional skills and competencies enables students to have less stress and anxiety at school and results in greater academic gains, positive feelings about self and school, the adults at school, and fewer disciplinary problems (Calderón, Slakk, & Montenegro, 2017; Durlak, Weissberg, Dymnicki, Taylor, & Schellinger, 2011). Approaching social and emotional learning from a whole-school perspective helps all students, not just Newcomers.

In Chapter 1, we discussed a plan of service that includes assisting with ELs' socioemotional well-being, and we'll now help you get started on the process and outline what you will need to consider. We will begin this chapter by sharing what one school does for their Newcomers, which is representative of that of other schools that we have visited. At the end of each subsection, we pose questions for your teams to discuss as entry points, and at the end of the chapter, we will present a rubric that you may use to help you track your progress.

Francis L. Cardozo Education Campus

When Newcomers enter the Francis L. Cardozo Education Campus in Washington, D.C., "the staff understands the complexity of issues that surround our EL population," Mr. Leonel Popol, bilingual counselor, explained to us and to parents during a meeting. All teachers are trained to integrate content and language instruction. The teachers work collaboratively to help students improve their listening, speaking, reading, and writing skills while creating a safety net for learning. The students:

- Learn English in every class. All teachers teach language within their content areas.
- Work in small groups in every class to develop trust and challenge one another.
- Engage in project-based learning to mirror expectations in the workplace.
- Interact with students from a range of cultural and linguistic backgrounds.

The International Academy also supports Newcomers with additional services to support the whole child and anticipates where support will be needed:

- Extended day for academic and social support
- Close communication and partnerships among staff and families
- Bilingual school counselors
- Bilingual social workers
- Health services

- Internships and community service opportunities
- Integration of social media and technology
- Programming through partnerships with community organizations
- Access to schoolwide extracurricular activities and team sports

Our visits to the International Academy leave us impressed on multiple levels. In its second year of operation, 92 percent of students met or exceeded expectations on the WIDA ACCESS 2.0 test. In the third year, they are working diligently to increase the percentage.

Recommendations from Cardozo and Other Schools We've Worked With

From interviews, we have collected key factors that cut across grade levels and multilingual groups. These schools typically assign committees to get started by keeping Newcomers' and ELs' home lives in mind, meeting Newcomers' health needs, and helping Newcomers with traumatic events or socioemotional needs.

Keep Newcomers' and ELs' Home Lives in Mind

Many Newcomers also have after-school responsibilities at home, such as caring for younger siblings or translating for their parents. To help them with critical translations, ESL programs can include language that addresses how to read and interpret forms and/or services the family might need.

Questions for your teams to consider when beginning to plan:

- How can the school assist with needed language and cultural support outside of school, such as help with "Basic Language for Families" to aid in communication during shopping, for home repairs, with landlords, or at doctor's offices, as well as various other basic necessities?
- What translation services are available to help with these so that the Newcomer doesn't have to miss school?
- How can the school facilitate and encourage community members to help Newcomer families with
  - —ESL classes for parents,
  - —Parent courses or meetings to understand the school's expectations, policies, and parents' rights,

—Job applications and placement services for parents, and

—Daycare services.

Meeting Newcomers' Health Needs

Researchers at the Migration Policy Institute (2016) have analyzed the myriad challenges faced by Newcomers. For instance, for the young ones, factors influencing early childhood development such as scarcity of food, lack of access to dentists, opticians, or other health providers may impact children's learning at school immediately but also manifest as gaps in later years of schooling. Challenges confronting older students may include health issues compounded by lack of medical attention, malnutrition, and the daily stress of caring for siblings or other family members.

As part of the registration process, Newcomer Centers typically provide information about community organizations that help with health care. Community organizations or health providers, dentists, optometrists, and counselors are invited to provide, on a monthly basis, services to address crucial health issues.

Two great examples are the *Success for All* schools and the *Talent Development* schools created by Johns Hopkins University researchers, which always require that the schools with which they work reach out to community health service providers. They enlist community providers to visit the schools, or even set up shop and be on call as needed. These two programs also require that there be a Parent Coordinator at the school to constantly reach out to parents with informational pamphlets in the languages represented in their schools. These Parent Coordinators also call or visit families when they notice that a student appears to have a health issue, needs glasses, or needs counseling.

As you ponder these examples, here are some critical questions your team might ask:

- Which local organizations can we enlist to provide training to our school and staff to be well-equipped observers of potential problems?
- How will the availability of these services be communicated to families? Are translators or translations available? Do we need to hire a Parent Coordinator? How can the whole school be more aware of our students' socioemotional needs?
- What can all teachers do to work together to provide a classroom and school environment where students feel supported socially and emotionally (as such support is essential for students to continue their academic growth)?
- What is the process to determine why a student is sleeping in class? Always late to school? Habitually disruptive? Never on task?
- How are teachers made aware of special circumstances and the support specialists who can help both teachers and students?

Helping Newcomers with Past Trauma or Emotional Needs

At various times throughout their journey, young and adolescent refugees often face violence, physical danger, and uncertainty that their basic needs will be met, along with the daunting task of resettling in a new country. Children in refugee families may have shared the journey's experiences with their parents or experienced degrees of atrocities alone. Children, even if born after the parents are resettled, may indirectly be affected by their parents' experiences: financial fragility; insufficient, unstable, or nonexistent housing; food scarcity; and community threats. Some research has highlighted the fact that ELs, upon entering the school environment and culture, often feel as if they are "caught between two worlds" (Igoa, 1995, p. 85) and frequently report feeling mentally and emotionally exhausted (Watts-Taffe & Truscott, 2000).

In a recent publication, we (Calderón & Slakk, 2018) also suggest a number of ways to provide services and reduce harm to children of detained and deported parents, including reaching out to health and human service agencies to assist in improving the staff's cultural competence and knowledge of issues associated with immigration status. (For more information, go to https://www.migrationpolicy.org/research/health-and-social-service-needs-us-citizen-children-detained-or-deported-immigrant-parents.) Counselors at Newcomer Centers/school counselors are well versed in helping students with these specialized needs and the requisite publications that also provide guidance, such as the Migration Policy Institute's reports, and often present summaries for the faculty to consider, discuss, and act upon.

The critical role of the school counselor and psychiatrist. The immigration literature also finds that when Newcomers arrive during high school years, it can be especially difficult for them to aspire to a college education, unless they have had adequate schooling experiences in their home countries. Otherwise, the EL may feel overwhelmed and prefer to concentrate on finding a job, which may result in the EL dropping out of school or failing to thrive.

Schools recommend discussions around these questions:

- How can our school counselors encourage universities and technical and community colleges to come and meet the students and parents and assist with applications, grants, and requirements for continued education and career readiness?
- How can our school counselors encourage community and business leaders to come and meet the students and parents and assist, through their networks, in finding them part-time jobs?

- What translation services are available to help counselors with student and parent meetings and to address academic, disciplinary, or socioemotional circumstances?

The role of counselors and teachers regarding stress disorders. If a student shows signs of or displays any of the following behaviors, it is important that the school counselor or the sponsoring organization assist in getting them professional help and treatment:

- Sleeplessness
- Having had/currently having nightmares
- Inability to get along with others, particularly in close relationships
- Paranoia and distrust
- Unwillingness to discuss or revisit in any way the site of the trauma
- Persistent, intense fear and anxiety
- Feeling easily irritated or agitated
- Having difficulty concentrating
- Feeling despondent or detached
- No longer finding pleasure in previously enjoyable activities
- Feeling helpless or "out of control"
- Experiencing intense survivor guilt
- Being preoccupied with the traumatic event
- Physical symptoms such as headaches, gastrointestinal distress, or dizziness
- Suicidal thoughts, plans, or gestures (in person or on social media)

Some students, despite having experienced these hardships, learn to survive, cope, and thrive. They have learned resilience.

Resilience characteristics. Despite difficult immigration experiences, Newcomers also bring expertise and resilience. Resilience traits include: adaptability, self-esteem, optimism, strength, and the ability to recover quickly. Researchers have found that participation in prosocial activities plays an important role in the resilience of Newcomer youth. In the immigration literature, youth with strong support networks (e.g., friends, family, faith communities) have been found to adapt more easily to their new culture and environment. They find that involvement in supported prosocial extracurricular activities, particularly with youth outside their own ethnocultural groups, can provide immigrant adolescents with potential role models, as well as valuable social capital and opportunities for integration (Zins et al., 2004).

Close friendships are important. Identifying a peer to welcome and introduce the Newcomer to other students and teachers speeds the level of comfort. Participating in extracurricular activities teaches social norms and provides opportunities for developing more friendships.

Developing Personal Coping and Excelling Skills

Newcomers can develop coping skills for events such as those identified by the Bridging Refugee Youth and Children's Services (BRYCS) once their teachers and school staff are made aware of these barriers and actively set out to build bridges for Newcomers. Classroom instruction and modeling can help them cope and excel as they run into such hurdles. Opportunities for peer interaction help Newcomers thrive academically and develop positive feelings about diverse peers, adults, and school in general. Nonimmigrant students will also develop knowledge, empathy, and support for Newcomers when they work with them in pairs or teams of four.

It is important to conduct pre-activity mini-lessons (see Figure 3.1) with modeling to teach the variety of general skills and related key language that a Newcomer or SIFE student may need. Skills and activities that we may think of as intuitive may be totally foreign to the Newcomer. Additionally, the nonimmigrant students in the classroom will also need to develop new acceptance, tolerance, and helping skills. There are five core social and emotional learning competencies (CASEL, 2018) that benefit all students. We integrated CASEL's competencies with the instructional components, as described in Chapters 6, 7, and 8.

FIGURE 3.1 When a Newcomer Arrives

✓ What mini-lessons might be needed before you can expect your Newcomers to be successful with classwork? When planning a lesson, consider the following:
  - How much education have your Newcomers had?
  - Will your Newcomers need help with everyday classroom tools? Holding a pencil? Using scissors?
  - What are the American educational system school norms?

✓ What subtle sociocultural or classroom curriculum elements might your Newcomers need help with?
  - How to share?
  - How to attend school or arrive on time?
  - How to speak with a teacher? With classmates? With other staff members?

Note: Many behaviors misinterpreted as "poor" were, in fact, never learned.

Recommendations for each of the five CASEL competencies as they apply to ELs/ Newcomers are as follows (Calderón, Slakk, & Montenegro, 2017):

1. *Self-awareness.* The ability to recognize one's feelings and thoughts and their influence on the Newcomers' and peers' behaviors, which includes assessing one's strengths and possessing a well-grounded sense of self-efficacy and optimism.
   — Working in Partner or Triad Reading lowers their affective filter and provides Newcomers a safe place to practice and stretch their newfound skills. It is safer to practice their new vocabulary, reading, and content learning with only one "buddy" rather than displaying their limited knowledge in front of a whole classroom. The buddy system helps them become aware of their progress and strengths as they prepare for whole-class and independent reading.
   — Nonimmigrant peers will need to work on recognizing how their behaviors influence the Newcomers' behaviors.

2. *Self-management.* The ability to regulate one's own emotions, thoughts, and behaviors effectively in different situations, which includes delaying gratification, managing stress, controlling impulses, motivating oneself, and setting and work-ing toward personal and academic goals.
   — When Newcomers work in pairs and teams, they need to first learn the lan-guage of the formal protocols and social skills that are necessary to work and communicate with peers. Posting, modeling, and then practicing social norms in the classroom before a cooperative learning activity will help all students refine the behaviors of self-management as they interact with others.
   — When teachers explicitly express high expectations as they present standards and goals, model the process and outcomes, explain the cooperative task, and monitor the cooperation of students, Newcomers will begin to focus on those goals and standards for themselves and monitor their improvements.
   — Nonimmigrant students will also learn self-motivation, how to control impulses, and manage stress.

3. *Social awareness.* The ability to take the perspective of and empathize with others from diverse backgrounds and cultures, to understand social and ethical norms for behavior, and to recognize family, school, and community resources and supports.
   — The ability to get along with peers is developed when students work in hetero-geneous teams of three or four as they apply social norms such as empathy,

contributing ideas, accepting others' ideas, compromising, offering help, and accepting help.

— Students also begin to apply these skills with family and community.

— All core-content teachers can help students become self-aware of their developing skills and knowledge. Teachers can use metacognitive Think-Alouds and modeling to help students recognize success, questions, and needs followed by opportunities for students to apply their knowledge and skills in a variety of academic areas and in problem-solving settings. Ongoing classroom debriefing of skills and performance assessment checklists can provide feedback about how a student's conceptual, analytical, social, and language development is progressing.

4. *Relationship skills.* The ability to establish and maintain healthy and rewarding relationships with diverse individuals and groups, which includes communicating clearly, listening actively, cooperating, resisting inappropriate social pressure, negotiating conflict constructively, and seeking help when needed.

— Students work in teams of four to formulate Bloom's-based questions before participating in a Numbered Heads Together whole-class discussion, where they will be responsible for responding on behalf of the team to answer questions. All members of the team will be under pressure, as all members will need to be ready to answer. However, with the support of teammates and the structure of the activity, all will learn to mitigate that pressure. They negotiate conflict constructively as they learn oracy and the civility of respectful discourse with transition phrases such as: *I respectfully disagree, I concur, I would like to add, Moreover, According to the author/text, and so on*, modeled and explained by the teacher beforehand.

— Communicating clearly is a goal that all Newcomers should be helped to adopt. They learn that listening actively and asking for help can help them learn English. They need to incorporate into their daily etiquette schema phrases for cooperating (more metacognitive modeling here works well) such as: *Can you help me? May I help you? Can we work together on . . . ?*

5. *Responsible decision making.* The ability to make constructive choices about personal behavior, social interactions, and school, which includes ethical standards, safety concerns, social norms, the consequences of various actions, and the well-being of self and others.

— During editing and revising, Newcomers will need help with vocabulary and grammar from more capable peers. During science experiments, Newcomers benefit from explicit instructions, partner summarizing, and understanding about safety. But, safety goes beyond the classroom; hence, it is important to point out safety concerns, and possible consequences via Think-Alouds and modeling or videos. They will also benefit from language such as: *I don't understand the next step. Is this right? I don't know how. I'm sorry. It's my fault. May I try again?*

The business sector requires these skills from everyone. As Newcomers' peers interact with Newcomers, they also learn the communication, cooperation, creative, and critical thinking skills necessary for life and career success.

School Routines and Expectations Unfamiliar to Newcomers and Their Families: A Ready-Made Curriculum Checklist

The Newcomer Tool Kit (USDOE, 2015) and the Bridging Refugee Youth and Children's Services (www.BRYCS.org) cite the following examples of stressful activities or actions for Newcomers or SIFE students:

- Sitting still for long periods of time
- Working independently or quietly
- Riding a school bus
- Discipline in the school context
- Physical exams and immunizations
- Following a schedule and rotating classrooms or teachers
- Attendance and report cards
- Using a planner
- Wearing or not wearing a uniform
- Changing clothes for gym in an open locker room
- Raising a hand to speak
- How students and teachers relate to and address one another
- Lining up to leave the classroom
- The role of school personnel and who to go to with specific concerns
- Co-ed classes
- What to do in emergency drills

The items listed should be part of the Newcomer curriculum for all incoming Newcomer students. Newcomers will need an orientation session in their primary language on what may seem to all of us as mundane or familiar to all students. U.S. school norms and expectations will be unfamiliar to students who have never been in U.S. schools. Teachers and school staff can approach these and other upsetting, jolting, or harrowing experiences for Newcomers with a few strategies:

1. Have conversations with the student. Identify a situation or issue and generate questions to begin to understand what the Newcomers know and how they feel.
2. Explain each routine's or behavior's significance to the student's ability to learn.
3. Analyze and integrate examples to support the issue.
4. Recognize the Newcomer's perspectives.
5. Be prepared to share the "other's perspectives" during appropriate times in the conversation.

Curriculum and Strategy Components: Cooperative Learning and Peer Interaction

A Newcomer might need the teachers to enlist assistance from peers or provide guidance on how to garner respect from classmates. Although reluctantly, Newcomers would welcome this care if it is done with empathy, modeling, and finesse. This is where Cooperative Learning comes in handy. There are numerous Cooperative Learning strategies for developing vocabulary, discourse, reading comprehension, and writing that also model respectful social interaction and discourse. Chapters 5, 6, and 7 specify Cooperative Learning strategies that are evidence-based. Some of these go along with teaching vocabulary and oral discourse (listening and speaking), others are better for reading comprehension (and listening and speaking), and there are very specific ones for developing writing skills (while developing more listening and speaking skills). In essence, Cooperative Learning scaffolds and supports growth in the four language domains—reading, writing, listening, and speaking—of second language, or any other language for that matter. ELs/Newcomers learn faster from listening and speaking, as they get assistance from peers while working on reading and writing activities in teams. Additionally, their peers learn more from helping others.

Although Cooperative Learning strategies produce many benefits, sometimes students and teachers shy away from them. Teachers may be reluctant to give up control of the classroom, but some learning chaos is beneficial for student success. If a teacher has good classroom management skills, norms, and a system already in place, there should be no problem with loosening the reins a little. After all, we are regularly advising teachers to let students be in charge of their own learning. Cooperative Learning strategies are part of the Gradual Release process students thrive on. Students who have not developed collaborative skills may either be reluctant to participate or prefer to exhibit behaviors that make students and teachers avoid teamwork altogether. Therefore, before starting work in teams, it is important to set the climate for cooperation by informing everyone about the process and that each will be held accountable for making sure everyone learns.

For example, when the teacher posts and reviews the cooperative norms—such as respect others, help others, accept help, be patient, use self-control—and has students rate themselves at the end of the activity, it helps all students develop socioemotional skills. Cooperative Learning strategies integrated into language, literacy, and content teaching/learning make it easier for all students to practice communication, collaboration, creativity, and critical thinking skills for better decision making.

The instructional strategies also benefit striving readers, students in advanced placement courses, and general education students. The instructional and professional components described in Chapters 5, 6, and 7 are based primarily on our experimental-control studies of the Bilingual Cooperative Integrated Reading and Composition (Calderón et al., 1998) and Expediting Comprehension for English Language Learners (ExC-ELL) (Calderón, 2007), as no other program for teachers/administrators of ELs has been researched and tested as much as these two models. The components apply to ESL, bilingual, and core-content classroom instruction and to the professional development models for a whole-school approach.

To help you and your colleagues assess your school's readiness to assist your Newcomers with more than just the curriculum, Figure 3.2 presents a rubric that a high school near a refugee center used as they prepared to receive incoming Newcomers. Their concern was not only amplifying their Newcomer Center but also wanting to know how to welcome these new students. The refugee center informed the school that the students came from three language background groups. No school staff member spoke any of these three languages. Besides hiring appropriate translation/interpretation services, they wondered what other steps they would need to take. Therefore, they plotted their approach in the rubric presented in Figure 3.2 and plan to add more examples of proof of implementation when they revisit and refine their plan.

FIGURE 3.2 Rubric for Socioemotional Awareness and Support

Process Component	Needed (planning notes)	Started (what else we need)	Successful (what we're looking for as proof)
What programs or processes do we use to get to know our Newcomers? • In the classroom • As a school community	*Our processes and procedures for this need to be reviewed as a team.*	*Teachers are encouraged to review Newcomer folders but need training on what the information means.* *We have culture night but could add an evening for Newcomers and parents to explain U.S. schools and customs.*	*Every teacher knows who their ELs and Newcomers are and at what ELD level they are.*
What community organizations and partnerships do we have to help our Newcomers feel welcome?	*Several churches help with resettlement and community services, but the school could partner with them to keep parents informed.*	*We have a dentist and nurse come to school periodically. We need to invite more health providers.*	*All teachers, staff, parents, and students know who to ask for help or where to look for help.*
Where are we with SEL competencies as a school community? • Self-awareness • Self-management • Social awareness • Relationship skills • Responsible decision making	*We need PD and a process for our teachers and counselors to recognize Newcomers' and other students' needs better.*	*We scheduled SEL PD for the first week that teachers return to work next year.*	*All teachers are comfortable identifying student needs and referring correct professionals in the school.* *Lessons include SEL components.*

4 Staffing Programs and Professional Development

You and your colleagues have just received your rosters for the new year. Many of you have noticed that there is quite an increase in the number of new ELs, specifically Level 1 Newcomers. You finally realize the reason for the PD and training this year, which is heavily focused on Newcomers and ELs. You are not alone. Nationwide, all classrooms are seeing an influx of ELs and an equally large number of Newcomers. At your first visit with the EL/ Newcomer committee meeting, the ESL/ELD teacher expressed his concerns over the slow progress of the current Newcomers. A few of the teachers who currently teach Newcomers said they wished they could do more, but the Newcomers are hesitant to participate in class discussions and activities. Another teacher said her two Newcomers were doing well in math operations but not the other subjects. The new school secretary wants to know how to help ELs' parents when they come in to register their children. The counselors would love to help but . . . . Everyone agreed they needed more how-to's to reach the Newcomers. You all have the same question: What professional development programs have positive outcomes for teachers, coaches, school leaders, and students?

We see or hear about the aforementioned situation regularly. The two typical issues the schools and districts experience are (1) not enough ESL/ELD teachers, and (2) insufficient comprehensive professional development for the general core-content teachers who will also be teaching one or more ELs. In many schools and districts, meeting staffing requirements seems a daunting task. It requires hiring new teachers and targeted training for existing teachers. Whether there are only a handful of Newcomers or a large new immigrant population in a school, the services needed by these students and other ELs pose difficult questions about staffing:

- How many ESL/ELD teachers are required?
- How many certified ESL/ELD or well-trained core-content teachers are required?
- If the current core-content teachers stay, what training will they need?
- How do we design an effective program?

We have gathered some great ideas from schools that have been recently impacted by large numbers of Newcomers or have been cited by the U.S. Department of Education-Office for Civil Rights (USDOE-OCR) and/or the U.S. Department of Justice (USDOJ) for not complying with staffing needs. As well, we are working on a Title III grant to study seven schools that are exemplary when it comes to EL/Newcomers' services and instruction. The following are some systematic ways they have addressed these questions.

How Many ESL/ELD Teachers Are Required?

For comprehensive guidance into staffing and supporting an EL program, we suggest examining the federal guidelines and tools found in the USDOE's Office of English Language Acquisitions English Learner Tool Kit, which can be found at https://ncela.ed.gov/files/english_learner_toolkit/OELA_2017_ELsToolkit_508C.pdf. It states that "Recruiting, developing, and retaining excellent educators is essential in order to ensure that EL program models successfully achieve their educational objectives. LEAs [Local Education Agencies] must hire an adequate number of ESL/ELD teachers who are qualified to provide EL services, and core-content teachers who are highly qualified in their field as well as trained to support EL students. These teachers must meet state requirements and have mastered the skills necessary to effectively teach in the LEA's EL program" (USDOE, 2015, p.31). The ratio of teachers to ESL/ELD students, though left to the individual states and districts, must be such that it will support the students in meeting the stated goals.

The number of ELs per ESL/ELD teacher varies, at times as few as 10 to 20 and as high as 50 to 60 depending upon the ELs' level of service needs. Federal guidelines, however, state that students should be grouped as follows, by proficiency levels in their ESL/

ELD and in content classes: students at Levels 1 and 2 should be grouped together and students at Level 3 should be taught by themselves or with students at Level 4, some Level 4 students who have good grades in the content areas can be grouped with Level 5, and some Level 5 students can be grouped with Level 6 students for direct service hours. However, they should be included in the general education classrooms for the rest of the curricular day when not having direct service hours provided. (See your district's guidelines for student-teacher ratios and grouping by proficiency levels.)

How Many Certified ESL/ELD or Well-Trained Core-Content Teachers Are Required?

Any core-content teacher who has one or more EL must be certified to teach ELs or endorsed to support ELs in addition to teaching their core content or participate in a comprehensive professional development program focusing on teaching ELs/Newcomers. School committees working on these issues found that the purpose for providing the necessary personnel is to effectively implement EL programs and thereby set the context for EL success. The number of staff is directly related to the number of students and the service hours required based upon the language and literacy needs of the students. Program and staffing planning should focus on the following:

- *Necessary personnel.* This includes ESL/ELD teachers who are qualified to provide EL services, core-content teachers who are highly qualified in their field *and* trained to support ELs, special education ESL/ELD teachers for dually identified students, trained instructional coaches who can support teachers, and administrators who can evaluate and assist all of these teachers. In many states, core-content teachers are now given opportunities to obtain an ESL/ELD certification. However, as is the case in Massachusetts, they must still participate in statewide professional development and ongoing licensure cycles-related PD focused on current evidence-based teaching of vocabulary, reading, and writing to ELs.
- *Professional development and training.* School districts, state agencies, and schools must provide adequate professional development and follow-up training to prepare EL program teachers and administrators to implement the EL program effectively and show proof of success.
- *Meaningful evaluation.* Administrators who evaluate EL program staff must be adequately trained to meaningfully evaluate whether ESL and core-content teachers are appropriately employing their training in the classroom in order for the EL program model to successfully achieve its educational objectives.

What Training Will Core-Content Teachers Need?

A quick search for schools and districts that are implementing PD for teachers who serve ESL/ELD students may lead you to Massachusetts and Virginia. As of July 2016, the Massachusetts Department of Elementary and Secondary Education (DESE) provided 60,000 teachers and principals with the Rethinking Equity and Teaching for English Language Learners (RETELL) Sheltered English Immersion Endorsement. Massachusetts' plan and implementation was the result of the USDOJ/USDOE-OCR's finding that the state failed to provide adequate service to its EL students. RETELL is now a state requirement to retain, renew, or advance an educator's teaching license. Virginia, however, opted to provide the training without inducement from the USDOJ/USDOE-OCR. The Virginia Department of Education's Office of ELLs opted to offer the ExC-ELL model comprehensive PD across the state. Virginia simply recognized the need and chose to meet the needs of their growing population of Newcomers. Since 2014, the state has two or three times a year offered ExC-ELL Institutes to teams of teachers and administrators from rural and urban schools. In 2017, three institutes were offered because demand was so high and so many participants signed up for the two Institutes as soon as they were posted. The 2018/19 school year will see a minimum of six sessions statewide with numerous school divisions, as they are called in Virginia, providing follow-up sessions in their schools for their own educators to make sure all teachers are on the same page as they prepare for current and incoming EL/Newcomers.

Designing an Effective Program: Comprehensive Training and Follow-Up at the School

Massachusetts' RETELL and Virginia's ExC-ELL are both based on the same design. Applying the instructional strategies described in Chapters 6–8, an ExC-ELL Institute trains participants in vocabulary, discourse, reading comprehension/metacognition, and writing skills integrated into each subject area, emphasizing an asset-oriented philosophy with high expectations for EL/Newcomers. We use ExC-ELL as a program example here. Although your district or school may choose another program, it is worth noting that ExC-ELL is based on research listed in the *What Works Clearinghouse* (USDOE, 2007) under the name BCIRC (Bilingual Cooperative Integrated Reading and Composition) and is recognized by the USDOJ/USDOE-OCR as an effective program for ELs. Whatever program you are contemplating, the basic components of ExC-ELL must occur in that program in order to be considered adequate (which is the term USDOJ uses for minimum compliance to ESSA requirements). Even though ExC-ELL is for any group of ELs and works for all of their classmates, one ExC-ELL Institute is geared toward Newcomers' instructional *and* socioemotional needs.

Comprehensive Training

ExC-ELL-targeted PD for teachers, coaches, counselors, school staff, and administrators, is designed to:

- Build a foundation of skills, knowledge, and expertise in teaching academic language, reading comprehension, and writing skills for ESL teachers;
- Build a foundation of skills, knowledge, and expertise in academic language, reading comprehension, and writing skills for all core-content teachers;
- Build knowledge and dispositions for addressing the socioemotional needs of Newcomers;
- Build knowledge that reflects a cultural orientation (that is, educators recognize the rich cognitive, cultural, and linguistic resources that Newcomers bring to their classrooms);
- Engage participants as learners during the workshops and provide participants with strategies that they can use to help their students learn content and language;
- Provide demonstration, practice, and feedback as part of the workshop;
- Provide lesson integration practice and use of student tools;
- Demonstrate performance assessment and student data gathering on learning progressions;
- Introduce the classroom observation protocol for follow-up at their schools with in-class expert coaching and feedback for the participants; and
- Introduce the classroom observation protocol for administrators and instructional coaches to evaluate instructional delivery and to gauge implementation progress.

In addition to the content learning at the workshops, this comprehensive model includes follow-up at the school via differentiated coaching, collegial activities, and teacher and administrator support systems in order to ensure transfer from training to implementation and a positive impact on the students and whole school.

Follow-Up at the School

Differentiated coaching by expert coaches. We have found that successful schools (see Loudoun County Public Schools, VA, later in this chapter) are those that provide coaching by expert trainers/coaches, district specialists, and site coaches in classroom for the purpose of:

- Modeling a strategy with students and to reassure hesitant teachers that the strategy can work;
- Planning lessons before coaching observations;
- Co-teaching with teachers who needed support initially; and
- Observing and giving feedback to the teacher who is more secure, focusing on strengths and setting goals for the next observation.

This type of coaching helps teachers move through the two-year loop at their own pace while meeting their needs along the way. Teachers with the disposition and skill to move quickly through the two-year loop—from declarative knowledge to procedural knowledge and, finally, to conditional knowledge, where they adapt their teaching to the classroom conditions and students' learning needs—only need a year of PD. Many teachers, however, require the full two years to effectively acquire the levels of knowledge and application. Experience is also not generally a factor in this process, as both experienced and novice teachers possess a range of knowledge, skills, and exposure to EL strategies that have not been proven effective. Expert coaches must therefore work with teachers as individuals: some teachers need to see the experts teach their class and others want constant technical feedback on their transfer of knowledge and familiarity with the new strategies and the performance of their students.

We have documented teachers' learning progressions through a cycle. This PD loop consists of the milestones as shown in Figure 4.1 and explained further in the steps that follow.

Learning to teach vocabulary to ELs is used as an example to detail a teacher's progress through the cycle, although it is used for the reading and writing components as well. Each phase is listed first, followed by the projected teacher outcome.

1. *In-Depth Professional Development Teacher Declarative Knowledge.* A teacher can talk about the why and what of teaching vocabulary but is not able to deliver quality vocabulary instruction.
2. *On-Site Modeling and Expert Coaching.* The teacher begins to work on a stronger instructional delivery after seeing vocabulary implemented in the classroom, using the strategies and receiving feedback.

FIGURE 4.1 Two-Year Professional Development Cycle

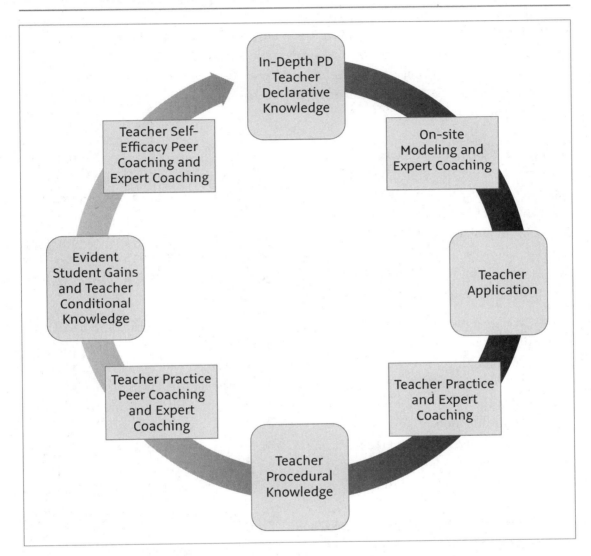

3. *Teacher Application.* The teacher continues to practice with frequency and fidelity.
4. *Teacher Practice and Expert Coaching.* The teacher receives more coaching from the expert trainers.
5. *Teacher Procedural Knowledge.* After sufficient practice and feedback, the teacher develops automaticity with the vocabulary steps.

6. *Teacher Practice Peer Coaching and Expert Coaching.* After more coaching, the teacher becomes confident with the vocabulary steps.

7. *Evident Student Gains and Teacher Conditional Knowledge.* The teacher sees the positive impact on her students and can now adapt the vocabulary steps and strategies to any group of students, any subject, and any situation.

8. *Teacher Self-Efficacy Peer Coaching and Expert Coaching.* After extensive practice and feedback, the teacher can now become a peer coach or a trainer of vocabulary instruction.

The WISEcard observation protocol. The Walk-Through of Instructional Strategies via the ExC-ELL card (WISEcard) is used by principals and assistant principals, expert coaches, and peer coaches (and by teachers themselves in self-evaluations) to observe a teacher's implementation of each of the 12 components of a well-integrated ExC-ELL model lesson and give or reflect on feedback to plan next steps. In addition to the expert coaches, the validity/reliability team, and the researchers who conducted the five-year study on ExC-ELL, teachers, literacy coaches, supervisors and administrators, and researchers found these tools useful for various other purposes:

- *Teachers*: As a template for planning content lessons that integrate language, literacy, and content; to record EL performance and track their progress; to reflect on the delivery of their instruction and how it correlated with the students observed during a given class period; and, by teachers observing and coaching each other, as a means of facilitating change, reaffirming effective practices, and sustaining motivation.

- *Literacy coaches*: As a means of familiarizing themselves with EL instruction when they needed to coach teachers of ELs.

- *Supervisors and administrators*: As a means of identifying quality instruction and rewarding teachers.

- *Researchers*: For conducting classroom research on fidelity of implementation, patterns of effective or ineffective instruction, and teacher-student learning connections.

After a few weeks of being observed and shown how to use the WISEcard observation protocol, the teachers began to use it to plan their lessons and asked peers to observe them and provide feedback. Often, they asked their peers to observe a few students in their classroom to get another perspective on their learning.

The WISEcard, and similar protocol observation tools, support systematic coaching and sustain implementation. Any tool that allows teachers to review, ponder, refine, and reflect upon their instructional practice can serve the same function as the WISEcard. Teachers who have been trained in ExC-ELL and then coached using the WISEcard will eventually be able to automatically review and assess their instruction using the target strategies. In the meantime, they have the support of the WISEcard and fellow educators to help them improve their craft. The WISEcard, or any other protocol observation tool, can be a source of evidence for the teacher to use to show growth and reflection on practice.

We designed the WISEcard to be an instructional aid to help the teacher with implementation, not necessarily evaluation by administration. However, teachers are encouraged to share their WISEcard notes and next steps with their administrators and fellow teachers. Loudoun County High School's principal stores the WISEcards for each of the teachers for the purpose of sustaining the momentum. This is her way of showing not only that she expects the WISEcards to be used, but also her faith that her teachers are self-reflective of their practice. She does not read them. She respects the teachers' privacy and does not want to be influenced when it comes to teacher evaluations. Teachers welcome the opportunity to use the WISEcards (as evidenced by the two teachers who we saw proudly walk in on a Monday to request that their WISEcards be added to their coaching files).

Teacher Support Systems for Transfer into Teaching and Learning

To set a context for the transfer from training, it is important to forecast for the teachers and administrators what would happen if, year by year, support for teachers is not in place. In short: implementation will erode and stop.

To ensure transfer from training into a teacher's repertoire and, thereby, result in positive student outcomes, we recommend that schools implement the following support mechanisms:

- All site coaches and administrators attend the institute on the instructional model, plus two follow-up days on ways to support teachers through their experimental phase and on how to use the observation protocol. This sends more than one message, but the main message is that the teachers see administrators and coaches at the training, learning alongside them as part of the team. As part of this step, administrators and coaches should communicate what they learned and what they expect to see as they visit classrooms.

- All site coaches and administrators shadow the trainers/expert coaches during some observations in order to develop expertise in the use of the observation protocol and proper evidence of implementation.
- Teachers working with dually identified students are also engaged in the training and coaching. (Note: In Massachusetts, the comment heard most often as a result of the RETELL training was that it was good for special education students too. One district in Virginia is planning on training special education teachers with the same strategies.)
- Highly proficient practitioners might be considered potential trainers and coaches and would receive additional training to continue to sustain the innovation. As site/district-based trainers or experts, they would train new teachers and conduct follow-up or review sessions on components teachers request throughout the year.

Coaches will need a basket filled with feedback tools. Feedback can make or break a relationship. It can build productive partnerships/teams when coaches have been trained along with the teachers, practiced new protocols, and have been provided feedback on their own coaching by expert coaches. Coaches have a difficult time coaching when the school district requires a coaching program that does not take ELs/Newcomers into consideration. Therefore, check the district's coaching requirements and programs and inform the district that your teachers and coaches will be integrating EL/Newcomer instructional strategies within that framework to provide specific feedback to teachers.

These kinds of support mechanisms flourish best in collaborative and cooperative climates (as we see in schools in Loudoun County and Stafford County, Virginia). Collaborative learning needs to be present throughout the implementation for teachers and students. Teachers work with colleagues at least once a week in Teacher Learning Communities (TLCs). In TLCs, teachers are engaged in sharing tips, modeling strategies that worked, and problem solving. These TLC activities, such as team planning, content alignment, and consensus on tiered vocabulary to teach, serve as a capacity-building exercise. These experiences are not only pragmatically important, but they also empower teachers to see themselves as active problem-solvers and continuous learners. Teachers use the WISEcard to account for fidelity to ExC-ELL teaching/learning strategies and for student involvement. Successes in a classroom, grade level, or content area are shared, celebrated, and replicated in other classrooms, content areas, and grade levels. At a Loudoun Middle School, a teacher writes herself in on the school schedule to indicate that she is either inviting teachers to come and observe her or wants to share successes in a TLC. Teachers celebrate and share successes in grade-level or content-area TLCs.

As expected, there are ups and downs in implementation. This is more evident when there is no evidence of student engagement and lessons are too teacher-centered. Sometimes the issue is classroom management. Regardless, questionable practices can be revised or discontinued as teachers share in their TLCs. Another option is for the school to request more workshops or more expert coaching to "help make things right." An expert trainer/coach can attend all-day content-level TLCs to listen to core-content teachers' concerns. Math teachers want to know how much vocabulary to teach in one period, which words to select, and how to combine reading and writing. Science teachers want help designing a rubric for writing lab reports. All core-content teachers want to become "language and reading teachers." Teachers just need time to get together and discover this wonderful world of teaching.

Beyond Language and Academics

Beyond the commitment and preparation for student academic success, there are now new challenges on the horizon. Educators must now ponder creating a "safe zone" for undocumented immigrants while keeping them engaged and motivated in their education. The socioemotional aspects that we described in Chapter 3 are part of everyone's learning. School districts can expect new waves of undocumented students. Hence, preparation can begin in TLCs' discussions. Planning should include ways to make students feel safe and that they belong in the school. California and other states have established themselves as sanctuary states/locations with educators partnering with local governments and law enforcement to find ways to keep the schools as safe zones. The U.S. Department of Education's website has additional information and resources on this at https://www2.ed.gov/policy/rights/guid/unaccompanied-children.html.

Support Staff, Electives Teachers, and Instruction Assistants Need Training

Frequently, we'll have a modern language teacher or two at one of our ExC-ELL trainings (which is great since the strategies we share work for any language, as they focus on academic language). However, when we train teachers and administrators, we rarely see teachers who teach band, orchestra, physical education, computers, media, or those who teach other wonderful electives and enrichment courses. This is unfortunate, since these teachers also teach ELs and have a curriculum that would benefit from instruction that also focuses on academic language.

At one school, a teacher told Shawn that he didn't understand why he was at the training session since he "didn't have any ELs." Shawn asked him what he taught. The teacher replied PE. This made Shawn wonder where the ELs were during physical education class. He asked if there was a different PE teacher who taught the ELs, to which the teacher replied that he was the only PE teacher. After several more questions about instruction and how many languages the PE teacher spoke, the light (and realization) began to dawn. The PE teacher finally said, "OK, I get it now." He realized that he did indeed serve all of the ELs in his school and that the strategies he was learning at the training would help in delivering his curriculum, even if it was PE.

In Royal Independent Schools, just outside of Houston, TX, every person who was in the classroom attended the ExC-ELL training and was expected to be able to work with the students using the vocabulary, reading, and writing strategies. In Stafford County Public Schools in Virginia, the instructional assistants did not attend the training. But because they assist with and observe instruction using the ExC-ELL strategies that their teachers provide to students, they are as proficient with the strategies as the teachers and can take over teaching tasks without a second thought if the teacher needs to step out of the classroom or is working with small groups.

As we recommended in Chapters 1 and 2, the front office staff and guidance counselors need training in intake and assessment. All members of the staff—cafeteria workers, nurses, custodians—have some connection to the students in the school, so shouldn't they know how to work and deal with Newcomers and ELs or, at the very least, know how to communicate with them or help them be safe? And what about volunteers? Are they not there to help all students? If they are there to help with curriculum and learning, then they need, at minimum, a primer on the strategies all teachers are expected to use. All staff members need to have some form of understanding of the whole school's commitment to every student's success and what their part is in it.

And last, but not least, off-site administration and support staff, coaches, and facilitators need to have information on the processes and instructional process they will see when they visit. This will need to include the rationale and evidence of successful implementation as well as formal and informal data to support the processes that have been put into place.

Collective Efficacy

In essence, the biggest challenge for a school is having everyone highly prepared to reach the Newcomers. When everyone participates in the same type of professional development and follow-up at the site, everyone's learning and successes accelerate. The positive mindsets toward ELs catch on quickly and the collaborative efforts turn into collective efficacy.

Nevertheless, it bears repeating that the moral commitment and love of teaching all children is backed by federal requirements. These requirements sometimes serve to propel schools, districts, and states into action. We therefore end this chapter with a checklist that can serve as a preliminary analysis of what is and could be.

The Tools and Resources for Staffing and Supporting an English Learner Program (2015) brief from the USDOJ/USDOE-OCR poses questions to help schools analyze their staffing and professional development needs.

As an example of a district committed to going beyond compliance, we have been working with and studying two middle schools and two high schools in Loudoun County, VA, whose Newcomer and EL populations have increased in the last four years. As is the case with schools in other counties in Virginia, there was a dire shortage of ESL teachers and/or core-content teachers with ESL credentials/certification. Then, in 2017, an additional opportunity came from a Title III grant to enroll teachers in a George Washington University ESL credentialing program—which would enable teachers, while they participate in the school's ExC-ELL professional development, school-based coaching, and TLCs, to also take courses toward their ESL endorsement. About 18 core-content teachers matriculated in 2017 and more in 2018, including some principals who wanted the certification.

Loudon County Public Schools, Virginia

Loudoun County Public Schools in Virginia decided to adopt the ExC-ELL program. They selected one middle school and one high school because they felt that the ELs in the upper grades needed more attention. For the first year, they decided to begin with half the teaching staff in each school. Seventy core-content, ESL, special education, and advanced placement teachers participated. The principals, assistant principals, counselors, and coaches also participated in the three-day institute with the teachers, and later in a two-day institute focusing on classroom Walk-Throughs, coaching, and establishing teacher support systems. Five directors and instructional specialists from the school district also attended.

The schools allocated 24 days of coaching by the ExC-ELL Master Coaches so that every teacher who participated would be coached several times. The principals, coaches, and three district administrators shadowed the ExC-ELL Master Coaches as they went to each classroom to observe and collect data using the Walk-Through of Instructional Strategies via ExC-ELL (WISEcard). Observations were reviewed with all observers afterward to ascertain validity and reliability. Additionally, the ExC-ELL Master Coaches debriefed with each teacher observed to get their perceptions of their lessons, give feedback on what was working and what needed to be improved, then jointly determined next steps.

In summer 2018, the remainder of the teachers from the middle school and the high school attended the institute, as well as school leaders and coaches who missed it the first time. District specialists were there again. Two days were devoted to the administrators' team to delve deeper into establishing the teacher support systems described in Chapter 4—how to observe classrooms with ELs and provide feedback to teachers and how to establish TLCs. These teachers were coached in the fall and will be coached in the spring by ExC-ELL Master Coaches and in-house/district coaches.

During the first year, the classroom observations highlighted that teachers typically needed help implementing the seven steps to preteach vocabulary. They tended to spend too much time explaining, thus going beyond the one-minute-per-word recommendation and providing little time for students to practice the word with their own sentences. Having another pair of eyes in the room to record teacher-student interaction helped them see where they excelled and where they needed to revamp. Using the SWIVL device to video their lessons helped teachers and coaches be more on target for next steps. Some teachers began by videoing themselves and watching the videos by themselves. After building confidence, they invited peers to observe them in the classroom.

The principals were so excited with the ongoing progress that they convinced principals from another middle and high school to implement ExC-ELL. The first cohort from these two new schools also began the professional development in the summer of 2017, and the second cohort began in the summer 2018. These two new schools are now going through the same implementation hill and valley phases that we previously mentioned. They learn from the specialists who also assist the original two schools, and they are now planning to schedule quarterly teacher-teacher and principal-principal meetings between the four schools next year.

Following are some of the comments made by administrators and students (noting that teachers' comments are not included, as they were all very similar):

Administrators:

- Exactly what a school like ours needs. It fits our vision and mission to improve literacy. It addresses all three levels of our students; Newcomers/ELs, Academic, and Honors/Advanced Placement. Every teacher can implement ExC-ELL. Our students will be able to use these strategies in college on their own.

- I like it. It provides an outstanding framework for instruction, whether in a self-contained SPED or ESL class or AP class and everything in between.
- Requires student engagement. Doesn't allow for passive learning. Gives them ownership of their learning.
- Makes teachers more thoughtful [in] planning and selecting materials.
- Teachers can adjust it to their content area.
- Teachers like all the literacy strategies that can be taught in the content area. Even when high school teachers haven't learned to teach literacy in the content area, they catch on quickly.
- There is so much student engagement and talking! No more sage on the stage.
- It's night and day to see kids working in an ExC-ELL classroom versus a class[room] where the teacher is doing something else.
- I would've loved to be doing ExC-ELL when teaching in high school.
- It challenges teachers' preconceptions of what students know. [Teachers] assume [that all students] know all that. [It's] not just ELs [who have learning gaps]. All our students have gaps, because we never stop to understand what they don't know.
- Helps us build a relationship with teachers.
- It's about kids' language and learning.
- Students see that they are growing in the moment.
- Next year, all teachers will have been trained at the school and they can meet in their cohorts. This teacher-to-teacher [interaction] will cement this in. [Teachers] can share how this works very well. [Teachers] going into their second year are getting better and more comfortable with it.
- Teachers are enjoying vocabulary and writing strategies but are still struggling with reading and after-reading strategies.

Students:

- For shy students or students learning English like me, it helps a lot.
- It's helping in AP classes to learn [the] background of texts.
- Easier way to learn.
- Vocabulary is simplified. I like the process. It's fun and others' thinking helps us.
- My English is a lot good. Still learning.
- All teachers should do this.
- Good for us. Some students can't say a word, so it's good to repeat and say examples.

- It's good. It's fun. We learn.
- I get to share my opinion and hear other opinions in math.
- It helps. We love to talk to learn.
- Helps to understand.
- It's good and fun. Helps us to learn.

Classroom Observations with the WISEcard

We collected observation protocols for each teacher using our observation tool—the WISEcard. Each school and the division's coaches and administrators collected additional WISEcard samples. The progression of observations tracks the progress for each content teacher. At the beginning of the year, most of the teachers struggled with the Vocabulary Step 6—getting students to practice using the new word with a peer. By the end of this semester, all teachers had improved, keeping to the 60 seconds of 100 percent student practice, the time allotment for Step 6, by using appropriate sentence frames (see Step 6 in Chapter 6), and coming up with creative ways of engaging students so they enjoy learning. Many who tried the writing strategies have seen improved writing. We have examined student products and can see the improvement. The primary challenge for a number of teachers in this division (and in other divisions/districts we've observed) is to try the Partner Reading plus Summarization and student question formulation. They shy away from it because they feel that adolescents will not like it or that it will be too difficult to manage. All expressed the need to see it again and to receive coaching on reading and after-reading components.

Classroom Videotapes

After analyzing videos of randomly selected teachers, preliminary analysis confirms that the majority of teachers are mastering vocabulary and the writing instructional components. A select few are implementing all of the reading components, with fewer implementing after-reading components. These patterns corroborate administrators' perceptions of implementation and the teachers' perceptions of their weakest areas, agreeing that the next steps for improvement are reading components. The teachers use SWIVL to videotape themselves and reflect on their lessons or share with other teachers in their TLCs to get feedback and figure out/plan next steps or refinements.

Unanticipated Outcomes and Benefits

Perhaps the most rewarding outcome and benefit is the engagement of all the school and district administrators and EL specialists/coaches. For example, at Sterling Middle School in Loudoun, Principal Gus Martinez, two assistant principals, and the instructional coordinators/counselors take turns visiting classrooms with us to observe and coach the teachers. After each observation, we compare data on our WISEcards and discuss how to give feedback to each teacher. A couple of days prior to the observation, the teacher requests the focus and time of the observation. Thus, when we walk into the classroom, we know what instructional vocabulary or reading or writing strategies we are to observe and gather information on what the teacher requests. This way, the feedback is specific and targeted to what the teacher is working on, which helps reflect on next steps. Most important, we find that this process is really appreciated by the teacher. Since the District EL Director and one of her EL Specialists also come to the schools we visit, they split up and accompany us as we observe classrooms, provide feedback to teachers, and debrief the school administrators at the end of the day.

School and district administrators have become expert observers of ExC-ELL instruction and great collaborators with our team. Their messages to teachers let them know that the teachers not yet trained are expected to be trained in the summer of 2019, which will result in all teachers implementing ExC-ELL in 2020, which will in turn benefit all students. The students are very comfortable with ExC-ELL-based instruction and all agree that it helps them learn better and faster. Six teachers have now achieved exemplary-level status and will be trained as part of a District Support Cadre for training and coaching other division teachers.

To help you plan and evaluate your school's staffing and professional development designs to adequately provide service to the newly enrolled Newcomers and ELs, see the rubric presented in Figure 4.2 (which got the four schools mentioned previously started). We have given a few examples of what notes might be made when completing the rubric. Thinking about the "Proof," what might you expect to see as evidence? Make some notes in the "Successful" column and check your responses with those that we provided in the form in the Appendix.

Further Implications

The foundation of your school's success is a well-prepared staff: teachers, administrators, coaches, front-desk staff, volunteers, and visiting specialists. The preparation for teaching

FIGURE 4.2 Rubric for EL Services Evaluation and Analysis

Adequate Number of Qualified EL Staff

Process /Component	Needed (planning notes)	Started (what else needed)	Successful (what we're looking for as proof)
Do all EL program, core-content, and special education teachers who instruct ELs have the appropriate certification, licensure, or training to teach ELs? If not, are they working to obtain it within a reasonable period of time?	Review all certifications.	Some teachers have attended EL strategy PD sessions, but the whole school needs training.	
Do all teachers who instruct ELs demonstrate the skills necessary to effectively implement the EL program?	An observation protocol would help us gauge implementation all around and quality of instructional delivery.	Classroom Walk-Throughs and coaching sessions will be scheduled throughout the year. Expert coaches are also scheduled to visit classrooms to provide continued support and PD.	
Does the Local Education Agency (LEA) or State Education Agency (SEA) provide supplemental professional learning opportunities, when necessary, to ensure that the EL program is implemented effectively?	Review PD offerings from the state and district. Evaluate need of teachers in our school.	The state DOE provides multiple opportunities across the state each year, but more of our content teachers need to attend.	
Do all EL program, core-content, and special education teachers who deliver instruction to ELs with disabilities receive PD specifically related to teaching dually identified ELs?	This needs to be a part of the initial assessment and plan for our programs and teacher development.	The state DOE is providing a statewide PD session for dually identified ELs. Several teachers are signed up to attend.	

Process /Component	Needed (planning notes)	Started (what else needed)	Successful (what we're looking for as proof)
Are the LEA's EL services adequately staffed with qualified ESL, bilingual, core-content, and special education teachers trained in EL strategies in order to meet ELs' language and content needs?	Our district sets these guidelines.	We have an ESL teacher shortage in our state. Some of our teachers are participating in state-funded endorsement programs.	
Are principals or other administrative staff tasked with evaluating EL teachers certified and sufficiently trained in EL strategies in order to meaningfully evaluate teachers who deliver instruction to ELs?	Our principals have been using the required evaluation forms. Now we need to find out how to use the WISEcard and how other school districts align both systems.	Our administration and leadership team will attend the ExC-ELL PD sessions with the teachers and the additional two-day ExC-ELL Admin. Academy afterwards.	
Are paraprofessionals, staff, volunteers, or others adequately trained to support ELs, and are they working under the direct supervision of a qualified teacher?	We need to make sure they attend.	After attending the ExC-ELL Institute, several teachers have been tasked with redelivering these strategies to our other staff members.	

Newcomers calls for simultaneously (1) employing evidence-based instructional strategies combined with social emotional support strategies and (2) providing teachers with support systems to ensure their success. Language, literacy, and content learning can be integrated with the appropriate approaches described in Chapters 5, 6, and 7.

The preparation for success entails both a comprehensive professional development program for all educators at the school site and follow-up coaching and collegial learning communities. Planning for successful implementation and support will be the most difficult of all efforts and in many respects is the most crucial. The tradition of seeking "quick fixes" or "doing to comply" or "using a set of fun strategies in any sequence" prevails in many schools that have a history of instructing ELs. However, we are seeing more caring and commitment in many schools/districts as they welcome Newcomers for the first time. They want to get it right from the start.

5 Schoolwide Programs

Your school's Newcomer/EL TLC and planning committee has realized that the final step is to pull all the pieces together, get as many stakeholders involved as possible, and focus on how to enlist the whole school and its community, including parents, with your plan. Part of that plan involves recommending that—before coming together as a whole school—four or five members from the Newcomer/EL TLC will each choose a chapter in this book and come together, jigsaw style, to plan and then present to the whole faculty what properly serving Newcomers and other ELs requires and will mean for all learners at your school. As part of that whole faculty meeting, each grade level or content team should debrief and create two questions they have and then put their heads together to discuss them as a whole group. After extensive discussion, the rubric at the end of this chapter can help your school pull together an improvement or action plan. With this checklist, the school can begin to see where there is a "Strong Implementation, Where We Are, and What We Need to Do."

Growth and Success

Whole-school success begins when the whole school does everything in its power to create a culture where everyone focuses on ELs, without neglecting other students. A wonderful benefit is that everyone in the school flourishes, including teachers. It continues when every teacher integrates instructional strategies, principles, and routines into daily tasks and collegial learning and sharing. It flourishes when the whole staff is being supported by each other and leadership to take risks toward adjusting practices and advancing individual growth.

In the whole-school approach to Newcomers' success, teachers, administrators, and staff work to make the school the dynamic point of change and success. When all teachers are tackling the same innovation, one they have never tried before—such as the instruction described in Chapters 6, 7, and 8—it puts everyone on the same page, and it creates momentum. This momentum sweeps every educator in the school into an ongoing journey. There will be no place to hide, because everyone is busy sharing in an open space where everyone can see everyone. Everyone will experience hills and valleys. Just as in anything new that we attempt, we get worse before we get better. Isn't that what we tell our students and own children? So, if we all believe that mistakes are normal, natural, and necessary to growth, we all grow together.

From Professional Development to Implementation

Many professional development programs come and go, but is there ever transfer? Typically, only 5 percent of teachers will be using what they learned in professional development a year later (Calderón & Minaya-Rowe, 2011; Showers & Joyce, 2002), and in the business world, the result is the same (www.businessperform.com/downloads/samples/TrainingToPerformance-Intro.pdf). Although transfer from training into the classroom and later into skills for the business community is a primary concern, important gaps in the research literature remain. The business sector seems to be much more preoccupied with transfer of skills, but it is still a rare concept in education. Therefore, professional development trends and workshops come and go, instructional fads appear and disappear, and little transfers into the teachers' active teaching repertoire. Worse yet, current teaching practices aren't improving students' academic success.

Teachers need to see that professional development on Newcomers and other ELs is not a fad or an add-on. Administration and instructional leaders need to show that it is an expectation and support its implementation. This whole-school, everyone-participating mentality is what will drive success for all in the school. The whole school will share energy and excitement about growth of self and all students. When all instruction follows a similar set of strategies and processes, students succeed, content moves along, and goals are attained. Inversely, when only a few teachers attempt the innovation by themselves, it typically erodes by the end of the year, and there is no significant effect on students. One of Margarita's first studies (1984) continues to hold true, as we have both observed over the years, finding that these patterns are exhibited from August to June: teachers come back from an August professional development very excited and start implementing new learnings, but reality soon sets in:

- There are too many other things that we are required to do daily.
- Our students complain because now they're being held more accountable.
- We have no time to plan lessons with new strategies.
- Our district/school wants us to implement another model.

Teachers begin to lose enthusiasm and motivation for the new approaches by the end of October. After Thanksgiving break, teachers come back reenergized and try a little bit again. After winter break, they are ready to try some more. Unfortunately, the worry over "tests" begins to drown out all efforts toward more practice, and it becomes more expeditious to revert back to old ways of teaching or spending unsuitable amounts of time prepping for the tests. Without expert and peer coaching for each teacher, we can forecast that nothing will change, as indicated in Figure 5.1.

FIGURE 5.1 **Forecasting Transfer Without Coaching**

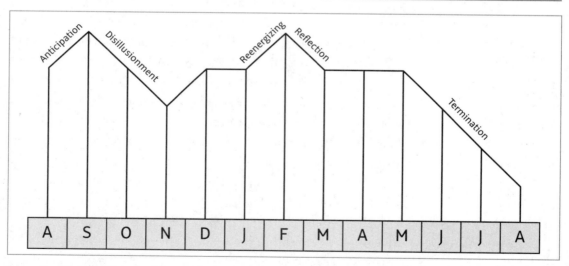

Source: From *Training bilingual trainers: An ethnographic study of coaching and its impact on the transfer of training* (Doctoral dissertation), by M. E. Calderón, 1984, in Dissertation Abstracts and Claremont Graduate School, San Diego State University.

In this chapter, we review the main components that make it all come together, ensuring transfer from training to effective implementation, to have a large effect on Newcomers, LTELs, dually identified ELs, and other ELs, while also addressing compliance.

Newcomer Programs

One of the most frequent questions we get is, "Which program works best for Newcomers?" Some districts have so few Newcomers that they just include them with the general education students and hope for the best. In contrast, some schools establish Newcomer Academies or Newcomer Centers. Centers can be at separate locations when there are large numbers of Newcomers continuously arriving in the district. Some centers work with K–5 students only, others with 6–12 or K–12. A center can be a school within a school or a separate school altogether, depending on the numbers. A center can be set up with 100 or more Newcomers. Having less than 100 Newcomers makes it difficult to schedule ESL/ELD and the content-area courses. These centers are usually close to the Newcomers' neighborhoods to provide them and their families with access to available resources, such as family health and social services. Regardless of how many students there are, all districts need a plan, a curriculum, and some form of intake program. Some centers have dual-language programs, and others have structured English immersion. All programs, big or small, center-based or not, must also adhere to the same federal requirements.

One important point to remember is that students cannot be isolated from general education peers. This means that after ESL/ELD with SEI or bilingual instruction, the rest of the day should take place in core-content classrooms. Some Newcomer centers for grades 6–12 bus their Newcomers to the closest Newcomer Center for half a day for intensive language, literacy, and socioemotional development. They are bused back to their neighborhood school for the content classes. Other centers have core-content teachers who are ESL/ELD certified to teach math, science, or social studies and the center is considered the students' home school.

To learn more about variations of academies and centers and their programs—and even plan a visit to one that shares your situation—visit the Center for Applied Linguistics at webapp.cal.org/Newcomer/.

When there are few Newcomers arriving throughout the year, a specific, self-contained ESL/ELD classroom with a certified teacher can be set up, along with selected core-content teachers who are prepared to shelter content through instructional strategies, as we describe in Chapters 6–8. Dual language and bilingual programs are ideal for Newcomers, yet these must be carefully geared to Newcomers' needs.

Newcomer Focus for Whole-School Reform

The following vignette, which details how one school is implementing follow-up to their professional development, is an example of how schools and districts have approached the implementation of a whole-school intervention and how to sustain it for positive outcomes.

A Middle School in Massachusetts

After professional development, this middle school in Massachusetts worked in Professional Learning Communities (PLCs). The teachers used three hours per week for what they called "powerful practice." They found that their ELD curriculum did not include sufficient basic classroom discourse. Going forward, they had one focus for the year—to study and implement structured student interactions. They planned how to teach ELs to actively listen and speak in classrooms. They gave ELs banks of language stems and inserted frequent "think-pair-share" opportunities, ensured partner summarization after reading each paragraph in a text, and used cooperative learning strategies throughout the class period. Once every two weeks, they visited each other's classrooms to observe these practices and gave each other feedback. When they met in their learning communities, they brought prompts, watched videos on the topic, and came up with new prompts. The school had different themes for PLCs focusing on EL instruction. One was on cultural differences. Another was on how to teach Newcomers dealing with entry procedures in the class, introducing the "do now" activity, and exit procedures. Other conversations focused on development of lessons that include emphasizing classroom norms and cooperative learning expectations that may be new to Newcomers or SIFE students who never attended school in the United States. These are the pieces of the hidden curriculum and expectations of going to school in the United States that other countries may not have or may do differently. Grade-level meetings were conducted frequently to talk about students of concern or family issues. At times, they also discussed the required curriculum map and pacing guide to give feedback to the administrators in the school and district.

In this district, the teachers noted that ELs were moving more rapidly through their WIDA levels and getting good grades in the general education classrooms. They were excited to see data from state exams.

Newcomer Center Versus School Integration

Depending on the number of Newcomers, and the decision-making setup of your school system, the school district may be the responsible entity to develop a Newcomer Center. However, in most schools, LTELs constitute 70 percent to 85 percent, and special education ELs, or dually identified ELs, about 10 percent to 12 percent of that school's enrolled population. Some districts have only 5 to 10 percent Newcomers. Your district may have an even lower incidence rate, in which case creating and sending them to a New-comer Center isn't warranted or feasible. Nevertheless, the ultimate responsibility for the correct service to Newcomers, ELs, and all students lies with the school itself. As such, a process/plan of action and/or mini-center for Newcomers may be warranted.

When Newcomers stay with their neighborhood school, they enrich the school, con-tribute to a global context where nonELs can benefit from participating in their cultures, sharing experiences, and learning other languages. Whether participating in a center or bilingual or immersion intervention, Newcomers and their ESL and general classroom teachers need a specific curriculum. There are now a few publishers who specialize in Newcomers' materials. In Chapter 7, we describe one that we are familiar with, because many ExC-ELL schools complement their instruction with RIGOR (authored by Dr. Calderón). A quick Internet search for "Newcomers curriculum," "Newcomer ELs," or "SIFE (Students with Interrupted Formal Edition) curriculum" will turn up others.

Building a Culture of Multiple Cultures

The students in your school are very different; so are your teachers. Revel in these rich differences. We find that cookie-cutter coaching practices do not always work, because every teacher is at a different place and is approaching innovation in a different way. Thus, we highly recommend that those who are coaching SEI or other ESL/ELD language and literacy strategies be fully versed in the strategies being coached. After a three-day or five-day session on EL and Newcomer instruction, the follow-up needs to be as versatile as possible. All teachers will experience the same training and afterward expert coaching. However, in addition to expert coaching, some teachers will feel more empowered to move into positive change when they have the options mentioned in Chap-ter 4 or in team activities such as those in the case studies provided in this chapter.

Seeking District Support for Better Assessments

New under ESSA, the school quality indicator aims to get at factors that may not be captured by the typical test- and metric-driven measures:

- Newcomer and other EL engagement
- Teacher engagement
- School climate and safety
- Progression of English language proficiency

- Access to and completion of advanced coursework
- Postsecondary readiness
- Rates of chronic absenteeism
- Graduation rates
- Socioemotional indicators (as described in Chapter 3)

All these factors impact growth for Newcomers. Most important for the whole school to keep in mind is that data must be disaggregated to show trends among groups of students (e.g., ELs, Newcomers, LTELs, SIFE) and racial groups. If the school is to dramatically reshape the system to be more inclusive and effective with all ELs, new and appropriate benchmarks for students, teachers, and administrators will need to be refined at the school level until better national measures are developed.

A challenge. The biggest challenge for schools with Newcomers and other ELs is the infrastructure. You need to show the disaggregated data on the range of ELs to the district. Here are some final questions to double-check and refine your plan to correct if needed: Are there sufficient ESL/ELD teachers? Are there enough funds for comprehensive professional development and follow-up coaching for all participants?

As suggested in this chapter, pointed and specific conversations on these pieces and other issues that you identify need to be brought up to the district. They, too, will be held accountable—as well as the state—for issues such as these.

A caveat. This professional development will need to be different from the usual. Some schools like to put professional development and/or curricula on top of existing curricula and professional development, which often contradict one another. Popular professional development programs for EL instruction might not be evidence-based because they are too shallow, have no follow-up plan, and haven't yielded positive outcomes. Some schools offer a few days of instructional strategies for teaching ELs just to check off compliance checklists. The teachers have fun at these workshops, but nothing transfers into the classroom. As enjoyable as these sessions are, if some of these professional development practices that have been around for years are still there, you might have to convince the district and EL specialists that the school needs a new approach.

Rubric for Schoolwide Implementation

In January 2015, the USDOJ and the USDOE provided joint guidance to ensure that ELs have equality in all educational classrooms. Their fact sheet to aid in compliance with ESSA regarding ELs provides the program guidelines that we have converted into the rubric in Figure 5.2. In short, education agencies are obligated to provide effective language, literacy, and content instruction in EL and Newcomer programs and general education classrooms where ELs spend most of the day.

Figure 5.2 is based on a case study of Lakeview Middle School in a southern state (name changed for confidentiality), where they have seen an extreme influx of Newcomers. Previous instruction and service to Newcomers was handled by the ESL teacher along with his other ESL duties. However, they have noticed an uptick in Newcomers arriving in their community. The district office informed them that they should expect even more Newcomers next year and beyond, as the district is growing and all schools are seeing larger numbers of Newcomers, as well as other ELs.

To summarize the key points of implementation from Chapters 1–5, the rubric in Figure 5.2 uses the USDOJ/USDOE guidelines for EL and Newcomer programs that you can share with your colleagues and entire staff as you begin this journey toward improvement. Use what you have filled in the rubrics in Chapters 1–4 to complete this rubric. This is a different style of rubric but serves the same function. As part of our professional development program, we provide examples customized to your school or district.

FIGURE 5.2 Rubric Based on USDOJ and USDOE Guidelines for Newcomers and ELs

A. Identifying and Assessing All Potential ELs

Strong implementation	Where we are:	What we need to do:
1. School/district has a process to identify ELs accurately and in a timely manner. Teachers and administrators know this process and act accordingly.	Front office staff acts as the registrar, enrolling students and alerting the ESL teacher when new ELs arrive.	New training for all office and administrative staff on how to enroll ELs. One staff member needs to be appointed as the registrar with another staff member as his or her backup. Designate one staff member and an alternate (most likely the Testing Coordinator) as the intake/assessment person. Registrar will notify administration, ESL teacher, and the Testing Coordinator (newly trained in the ESL intake/assessment process) Testing Coordinator will coordinate with the ESL department on screening and placement.

continued

A. Identifying and Assessing All Potential ELs (*continued*)

Strong implementation	Where we are:	What we need to do:
2. School/district must then determine if potential ELs are in fact ELs through a valid and reliable test that assesses English language proficiency in speaking, listening, reading, and writing. Teachers and administrators know which students are highly schooled newcomers, unaccompanied minors, homeless ELs, long-term ELs, Students with Interrupted Formal Education, special education ELs, and reclassified ELs.	Students are scheduled with any teacher who has available space in their class and for pull-out sessions with the ESL teacher.	Testing Coordinator will assess the incoming students for proper ELD levels and inform the assistant principal overseeing the ESL department and the ESL Language Instruction Educational Plan (LIEP) chair. LIEP chair and AP will review students' ELD levels and recommend the most appropriate level of service and program.

B. Staffing and Providing Language Assistance to ELs Available

1. Appropriate ELD/ESL services for ELs at different levels of listening, speaking, reading, and writing proficiency and background factors (unaccompanied newcomers, highly schooled Newcomers, long-term ELs, etc.).	Students are with any teacher who has available space in their class and are available for pull-out sessions with the ESL teacher as called for based upon their level of direct service hours.	LIEP chair and AP will review students' ELD levels and recommend number of service hours, appropriate staff members, and class/teacher assignment and schedule.
2. All core-content, electives, bilingual, special education, and specialty teachers use exemplary practices for integrating language, literacy and content (i.e., ExC-ELL).	The ESL teacher provides ESL curriculum and helps general content teachers as requested. Some teachers have received their ESL endorsement.	Whole-school staff training (an ExC-ELL Institute) to infuse best strategies and practices in all classroom for all ELs scheduled as part of end-of-year PD and opening-of-school PD next year. LIEP-focused TLC to work with all teachers to implement, coach, and infuse academic language strategies presented at the ExC-ELL training.

Strong implementation	Where we are:	What we need to do:
3. All core-content, ELD, ESL, SEI, bilingual, and special education teachers base their lessons on language standards.	All teachers are expected to post standards and objectives for every lesson.	Teachers will post, explain, and discuss both standard-based content and language objectives for lessons and activities. Content and language objectives will be reviewed at the end of each lesson with students to help them see where they are succeeding.
4. All teachers are qualified to teach ELs and administrators to lead the school toward successful EL instructional strategies implementation.	Some teachers have received their ESL endorsement. Some teachers have been trained in WIDA and SIOP.	Whole-school staff training (an ExC-ELL Institute) to infuse best strategies and practices in all classroom for all ELs scheduled as part of end-of-year PD and opening-of-school PD next year.
5. School has highly qualified ESL/ELD and core-content teachers and support personnel prepared to address educational needs of ELs.	Some teachers have received their ESL endorsement. Some teachers have been trained in WIDA and SIOP.	The district has provided an additional ESL position for the upcoming school year and has established guidelines for an EL/LIEP department, committee, and department chair to facilitate service and scheduling decisions. The LIEP committee will need to discuss and review ELs' ELD levels, service hours, testing modifications, and academic progress. The committee will also advise the intervention team as needed regarding any possible special education services or socioemotional supports.
6. Administrators and teachers of core content, specialties, and electives continuously attend PD sessions to update their skills for integrating vocabulary, discourse, reading, writing, cooperative learning, and instruction for socioemotional support into their subject areas.	Some teachers have regularly attended district or district or state-sponsored WIDA, SIOP, or ExC-ELL trainings.	A Renew, Revisit, and Refresh one-day session is scheduled for the spring semester. The LIEP TLC will meet regularly to revisit, model, coach, and help with implementation of ExC-ELL strategies in all classrooms. Grade- and content-level meetings will provide time to share successes and to work through ExC-ELL implementation in the general education classroom.

continued

FIGURE 5.2 Rubric Based on USDOJ and USDOE Guidelines for Newcomers and ELs *(continued)*

B. Staffing and Providing Language Assistance to ELs Available

Strong implementation	Where we are:	What we need to do:
7. School has established Learning Communities for teachers to share lessons, model strategies, and discuss EL progress. School provides supplemental training when necessary.	Grade- and content-level teams meet monthly to discuss/plan content and student progress. Co-teachers meet regularly to plan joint lessons.	An LIEP TLC committee will meet monthly, as stated previously. Co-teachers are given planning time once a week.
8. Schedule a comprehensive professional development program and follow-up with specific activities for the next two years.	The School Improvement Plan lists ESL standards and expectations.	Administration, LIEP committee chair, and grade-level and department chairs will meet to plan continuing PD and ways to train new staff members, and to support continued implementation from year to year.

C. Providing Meaningful Access to All Curricular and Extracurricular Programs

1. ELs have access to grade-level curricula so that they can meet promotion and graduation requirements.	Students attend regular classrooms with ESL support. ESL teacher helps with content when general ed teachers request assistance and help plan their co-teaching lessons.	All staff will be trained in ExC-ELL strategies to help all students succeed. LIEP committee will review student progress quarterly.
2. ESL/ELD materials are age appropriate and address CCSS standards.	We use the district-provided materials and pacing guide.	Additional ELD-level training will be provided to help core-content teachers scaffold and support grade-level content. ExC-ELL implementation will help with differentiation.
3. ELs participate in all programs: magnet, gifted and talented, career and technical education, arts, athletics programs, advanced placement, International Baccalaureate courses, clubs, and honor societies.	ELs' elective classes are with their ESL teachers except for PE, technology, and band/orchestra. All sports are open for all students to try out.	All students will be informed of all available courses including modern languages, IB, and other electives. All announcements for sports, clubs, and academic and after-school programs will be provided in Spanish and other L1 languages, as appropriate.

D. Avoiding Unnecessary Segregation of ELs

Strong implementation	Where we are:	What we need to do:
1. While receiving separate instruction for a limited portion of the day for targeted ESL, ELs have access to core content and curricular and extracurricular activities. (Typically, Level 1 and 2 students receive 2 hours of ESL, Level 3 students receive 1 1/2 hours, and Level 4 and 5 students receive 1/2 hour of ESL a day, although it varies by state. ELs should spend the remainder of the day in core-content and extracurricular activities with general education students.)	The ESL teacher has students for one period per day unless they are ELD/WIDA Levels 4 or 5. For high ELD levels, the ESL teacher pushes in several times a week.	The LIEP committee and chair will review and adjust as needed each student's service hours and ELD levels to conform to state-mandated guidelines.

E. Evaluating ELs for Special Education and Providing Dual Services

1. ELs are identified, located, and evaluated for special education in a timely manner.	The ESL teacher and general ed teacher confer and meet with the Intervention team as needed.	The LIEP Chair or designee will work with the special education department to assess and monitor the needs of current and possible Dually Identified ELs.
2. EL students with disabilities are provided both the language assistance and the disability-related services to which they are entitled under federal law.	Special education teachers set the schedule for their caseload based upon each student's IEP.	Keeping in mind that special education and ESL services hold equal importance and one does not supersede the other, the special education and ESL departments/chairs or designees will: a) work to establish proper accommodations and service hours to be included in each dually identified EL's ELD level and IEP. b) work with the core-content teachers to provide an equitable and appropriate schedule based on the student's ELD level and IEP

continued

FIGURE 5.2 Rubric Based on USDOJ and USDOE Guidelines for Newcomers and ELs (*continued*)

E. Evaluating ELs for Special Education and Providing Dual Services

Strong implementation	Where we are:	What we need to do:
3. ELs are evaluated in an appropriate language-based assessment on their needs and language skills, and the team designing their plan includes ESL/ELD personnel.	The ESL teacher has been helping teachers with accommodations and modifications. Dually identified ELs are assessed using the *Alternate ACCESS for ELs* assessment.	Keeping in mind that special education and ESL services hold equal importance and one does not supersede the other, the special education and ESL departments/chairs or designees will work with the Testing Coordinator to provide the most appropriate testing accommodations and setting based on the student's ELD level and IEP.

F. Monitoring and Exiting EL Students from EL Programs and Services

1. Exited ELs are monitored to ensure language proficiency and content knowledge within a reasonable time.	The ESL teacher checks with core-content teachers on student progress.	The LIEP committee will review the progress of all exited ELs for at least four years per DOJ/DOE-OCR and district guidelines. Documentation of this review and appropriate remediations or additional support will be provided to each student's teachers, placed in the students LIEP cumulative folder, and reviewed with the student and parents.
2. School has specialized courses and activities to help long-term ELs access grade-level core content.	The ESL teacher has after-school tutoring for those who want to come.	Whole-school staff training (an ExCELL Institute) to infuse best strategies and practices in all classrooms will help teachers and long-term ELs to succeed.
3. Compensatory services and differentiated intervention programs are offered with after-school or Saturday activities to help ELs accelerate their learning.	The ESL teacher has after-school tutoring for those who want to come.	Each grade level and content team will have at least one teacher or volunteer for additional after/before school or Saturday tutoring. The district will implement a summer institute for ELs who wish to attend. Although all ELs are eligible to attend, the focus will be on gateway grades.
4. Opt-out ELs are monitored for their progress and are offered services if struggling.	We have no opt-out students at this time.	The LIEP committee and a member of the administration team will formulate a plan for any possible future opt-out students.

G. Ensuring Meaningful Communications with Limited English Proficient Parents

Strong implementation	Where we are:	What we need to do:
1. Parents are informed of their rights in a language they understand regarding the range of EL services that their child could receive and the benefits of such services.	The ESL teacher sends out the district-provided parent letter when a student is classified as an EL. Parents also receive a copy of the yearly ACCESS Parent Report.	ACCESS Parent Reports and information letters will be sent out in the parent's primary language. Translators will be available for the LIEP Chair, Testing Coordinator, or ESL teacher to help parents understand ESL services, testing, and student rights.
2. All information is translated into the family's home language(s) and interpreters are provided as necessary.	Some letters, announcements, and flyers are translated into Spanish upon request. The ESL teacher, who speaks Spanish, translates for general ed teachers when requested to do so for calls home.	The district will be implementing an interpretation service for each school to use when communicating with parents. District guidelines for the coming year will require that a translator to be provided for parent-teacher conferences, curriculum nights, or any parent conference. Major school communications will be provided in the top five languages on the school's website.
3. School evaluates the professional development program currently in place, evaluates the transfer from the training, and the frequency, fidelity, and quality of the implementation. If it is not effective, it needs to be improved.	Some teachers have attended district-provided WIDA, SIOP, or ExC-ELL trainings.	LIEP committee and administration will review the number of new staff members for the coming year and observation data to determine the type of PD needed for the following year. Possible sessions are Renew, Revisit, and Review of ExC-ELL, ExC-ELL 10 (for those new to ExC-ELL), site-based ExC-ELL coaching, training, and/or curriculum and lesson implementation planning sessions.

Source: Calderón, Slakk, & Montenegro (2017).

Next Steps

In Chapters 6, 7, and 8, we describe instructional practices that have led schools in Loudoun County, Massachusetts, and many schools across the country to begin their paths toward a whole-school approach that creates powerful learning and great outcomes for all students and adults.

6 Teaching Vocabulary and Discourse

- *EL students are entitled to appropriate language assistance services to become proficient in English and to participate equally in the standard instructional program within a reasonable period of time.*

- *School districts can choose among programs designed for instructing EL students provided the program is educationally sound in theory and effective in practice (US-DOJ & USDOE, 2015).*

We can address diverse language levels of Newcomers and other ELs. All benefit from vocabulary instruction that develops listening, speaking, reading, and writing skills and content knowledge. Here is a way to begin integrating vocabulary into reading, writing, and content skills development. We present 12 key components of instruction where vocabulary/academic language can be introduced and practiced.

The 12 Components of Effective Instruction for Newcomers and Other ELs

This chapter describes the Expediting Comprehension for English Language Learning (ExC-ELL) empirical study, which was based on a five-year research project encompassing academic language, reading comprehension, and writing skills within each subject area as the best way to provide quality instruction for ELs. It was developed to be implemented in schools with ESL/ELD, Structured English Instruction (sometimes called Sheltered English Instruction), and Dual Language classrooms. ExC-ELL consists of 12 components (see Figure 6.1) that can be taught in sequence to help Newcomers and other ELs learn English and content simultaneously to expedite their learning (Calderón, 2007; Calderón, Slakk, & Montenegro, 2017; Calderón & Slakk, 2018). In this chapter, we focus on the vocabulary/academic language and discourse component and strategies to be infused into classroom instruction and lessons. In Chapters 7 and 8, we elaborate on reading and writing instructional strategies, respectively, and how vocabulary and content are embedded. The USDOJ and the USDOE approved the use of the ExC-ELL components in the RETELL instructional model that was used to train 60,000 educators in Massachusetts to meet compliance with the USDOJ.

FIGURE 6.1 **The 12 Components of ExC-ELL**

 1. Preteaching of vocabulary
 2. Teacher Think-Alouds
 3. Student peer reading
 4. Peer summaries
 5. Depth of word studies/grammar
 6. Class debriefings/discussions
 7. Cooperative learning strategies
 8. Formulating questions and numbered heads
 9. Roundtable reviews
10. Prewriting and drafting
11. Revising/editing
12. Reading final product

For the ExC-ELL Lesson Integration Tool template and other tools, go to ExC-ELL.com.

A research methodology called "components testing" was used to compare and contrast instructional strategies for vocabulary, oracy, reading, writing, cooperative learning, and content learning. Each component application was done separately (Calderón, 2007). For instance, by testing one vocabulary approach with another, we could see which one worked better with the diversity of ELs and the general education students who were in their classrooms. When we did not find an approach that could be proven to work better for ELs, we developed our own. We then worked out the bugs before integrating vocabulary, reading, and writing into a lesson. The integration phase was also tested before the final model was implemented and more student data was gathered from

ExC-ELL schools and compared to models being implemented in other schools. We continue to analyze and refine these strategies with each training session and coaching visit.

As these components and strategies focus on academic language acquisition, they are easily implemented in any instructional setting, in any language, and at any level of schooling, from kindergarten through university. Professional development sessions completely in Spanish, known as Accelerando la Comprensión en Español: Lectura, Escritura y Razonamiento Academico (ACE-LERA), have been held for New York City, Texas, Puerto Rico, and Latin American countries. Additionally, while implementing the RETELL professional development in Massachusetts, teachers frequently found that the ExC-ELL-based strategies also worked for special education and remediation students.

Cycle of Instruction for Meeting Planning Goals

When vocabulary, reading comprehension, and content-based writing work together as a unit, they are cyclical in nature. Vocabulary learning assists reading comprehension, reading comprehension aids writing, writing shows proof of content consolidation and mastery, and content mastery and writing calls for specificity and more complex vocabulary learning and usage.

Figure 6.2 shows the 12 ExC-ELL components as a circle. Note that each component adjusts, aids, supports, and connects with, as needed, each of the other components, the learner, and the lesson to strengthen and advance language acquisition and content mastery.

The Keystone Component: Vocabulary

Each and every student benefits from access and exposure to more Tier 2 and Tier 3 words, enabling them to comprehend the subject-matter texts, conduct rich discussions around those texts, write cohesive text-based assignments, and do well on state standards tests. By "texts" we mean any text students read in any subject. It can be online or a regular textbook, trade book, novel, or document. Additionally, directions for activities, tests, or experiments are included in this meaning of "text." Furthermore, any compilation of words students are expected to process should be considered a "text," inclusive of videos or songs. Naturally, the Newcomers also need Tier 1 along with Tiers 2 and 3. They need to be taught Tier 1, Tier 2, and Tier 3 words concurrently from the onset. Focusing on only Tier 1 easy words delays their progress.

"Tier 1, 2, or 3 words?" Isabel Beck and colleagues in 2003 and 2005 defined vocabulary words in tiers based on occurrence in reading and the instructional need to provide

FIGURE 6.2 Components of a Vocabulary, Reading, Writing, and Content-Infused Lesson

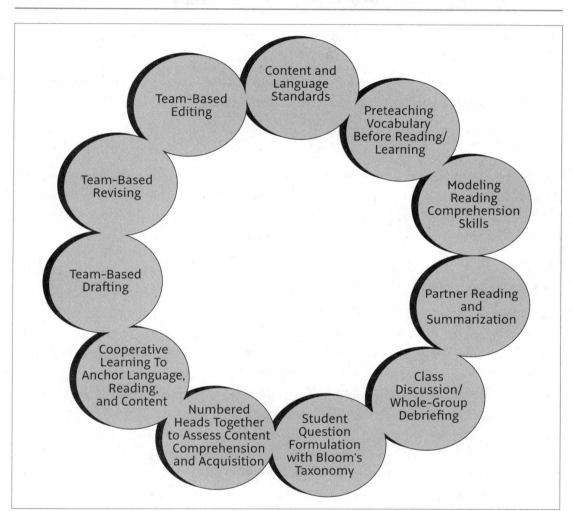

Source: From *Preparing math, science, social studies, and language arts teachers with English learners with ExC-ELL: Report to the Carnegie Corporation of New York* by M.E., Calderón, A. Carreón, D. Duran, & A. Fitch, 2009, New York: The Carnegie Corporation of New York. 2009 by The Carnegie Corporation of New York. Used with permission.

meaning based on usage and frequency (see Figure 6.3). Beck describes Tier 1 words as basic words that rarely require instruction. Tier 2 words are high-frequency words that have multiple cross-disciplinary meanings. These are the words that help us to define and comprehend the subject-specific Tier 3 vocabulary. Tier 3 words are those that are highly specific to content and are rarely used in more than one subject area.

FIGURE 6.3 Three Tiers for Newcomers

Tier 3. Subject-specific words that label content-discipline concepts, subjects, and topics; infrequently used academic words.

Tier 2. Information-processing words that nest Tier 3 words in long sentences; polysemous words, transition words, connectors; more sophisticated words for rich discussions and specificity in descriptions.

Tier 1. Basic words ELs need to communicate orally, read, and write.

Source: From Choosing words to teach. In E. H. Hiebert & M. L. Kamil (Eds.), *teaching and learning Vocabulary* (pp. 207–222), 2005, Mahwah, NJ: Lawrence Erlbaum. Copyright 2005 by Lawrence Erlbaum. Used with permission.

We have found that the most effective vocabulary instruction for ELs focuses on Tier 2 words and phrases to comprehend Tier 3 words and phrases that are typically defined in a text. However, Newcomers, who may be in a formal educational setting for the first time, will need assistance with Tier 1 words as well.

Where Do These Words Come From?

Upon arrival at the school, Newcomers need to be shown and taught their survival phrases (e.g., *lunch room, help, thank you, I feel sick,* and *I need help*) in writing so they get used to reading. These phrases can and should be part of your Newcomer curriculum. This will help assess further their basic reading skills needs (e.g., knowing the alphabet, phonemic awareness, phonological awareness, word meaning, and comprehension). They should practice reading the new words and phrases and saying them. At the same time, Newcomers *can* learn Tier 1, Tier 2, and Tier 3 words when these words come from the text(s) they are about to read. *Yes, Newcomers can start to read from day one,* if five key Tier 1 or Tier 2 words or phrases are taught before reading. These five words are only a precursory entry into reading. In Chapters 7 and 8, we describe what explicit instruction follows the preteaching of the five key words for each piece of text.

Newcomers in all grade levels can read ESL, language arts, social studies, science, and math texts. Even in secondary schools and Newcomer Centers, their content texts can be at a simple-language level dealing with subject-matter Tier 3 words, as well as the Tier 1 and 2 words that nest the Tier 3 words. The Benchmark Education Company has a huge selection of science, social studies, math, and language arts books that are ideal for Newcomers at all grade levels (www.benchmarkeducation.com).

We know from research (National Academies of Sciences, Engineering, and Medicine, 2017) and our own implementation studies that Newcomers *can start speaking, writing, listening, and reading from day one* when teachers use the tools and strategies described in this chapter and in Chapters 7 and 8. In actuality, all ELs should and can participate in the content and classroom by speaking, writing, listening, and reading every day and in every class. We suggest starting the process with preteaching vocabulary to give them a base from which to start, thus enabling them to quickly move into reading and writing. Learning a language and academic achievement no longer has to be delayed.

> At an elementary school in Charlotte, North Carolina, Shawn observed the progress of one 5th grade student (we'll call him Rodrigo) who arrived at the beginning of the year with an ELD level of 1.1—basically zero English. Rodrigo was immediately included in all classroom activities from day one. In the beginning, he merely repeated what his partners and classmates said, phonetically read the text with partner assistance, and copied sentence frames as part of the writing activity. Soon, however, Rodrigo was expressing his own opinions and creating his own answers orally and during the writing activities. By the end of the year, even though he was exempt from some of the tests, Rodrigo wanted to take them to see how far he had progressed. He came within two points of passing. Later, Rodrigo's composite WIDA score showed that his ELD level went from 1.1 to 3.4. Granted, Rodrigo was highly educated in Ecuador, and thus he had a good grasp of the content. However, he is not alone in this level of success when the expectation is that every student will participate and succeed in the classroom.

Over the years, several myths have persisted that have negatively impacted all ELs. The hypothesis that there is a silent period for ELs is just that, a hypothesis. There is no empirical evidence that proves it works. Case in point, our young man Rodrigo. Conversely, we have evidence-based studies that demonstrate effective learning of English and grade-level competencies can be accomplished *not* in 7 to 10 years but in 2 or 3 years at the elementary schools (Calderón, Hertz-Lazarowitz, & Slavin, 1998; Slavin, Madden, Calderón, Chamberlain & Hennessy, 2011) and at the secondary schools (Calderón, 2007) when teachers are given the tools to create a safe classroom context to immediately initiate speaking, listening, reading, and writing for Newcomers.

We have studies of whole-school endeavors where teaching Tiers 1, 2, and 3 vocabulary from texts students read became the cornerstone for the year's amazing growth in reading and math (Calderón & Minaya-Rowe, 2011; Calderón, Slakk, & Montenegro, 2017). One of those was a middle school in Washington Heights in New York City with a 90 percent Language Minority population. The school had been reconstituted with new teachers and a new principal. The principal brought us to the school to conduct professional development and coaching for all the teachers. After two years of implementing the 12 ExC-ELL components, the school went from lowest to highest performing in the district. New York City designated it as an exemplary demonstration school so that other schools could come and learn from their implementation. The school began by using the 7 Steps (for Preteaching Vocabulary (the "7 Steps") to teach Tier 2 words or phrases selected from each content text. Soon, core-content teachers reported that all their students were benefiting from the 7 Steps. This immediate success became the impetus for moving into the rest of the 12 components. By the end of the first year, the majority of the teachers were implementing the 12 components as best they could. It took another year to solidify sustainability. The students continued to excel, and the school kept getting top grades.

In Figure 6.4, the first words on the list for each function (e.g., *cause and effect, contrast, addition or comparison, giving examples*) can be used by Newcomers during the first month that they are in school. For example, when talking about or writing about *cause and effect,* the Newcomer can be taught to use the word *because.* However, the following month, a new transition word should be required for all oral and written discourse (e.g., *due to, as a result,* or *since*). The subsequent month, new transition words should be introduced and used in all learning events. Notice the transition to phrases? Phrases should be taught as a cluster. Thus, each month, new words or phrases are introduced and used. This is the best way to keep track of each student's learning progression. It also instills in each student the mindset that the onus is on them to learn new words or phrases day by day, week by week.

FIGURE 6.4 Selecting Words or Phrases to Preteach from Student Texts: Tier 2 Words and Phrases

Cause and effect: because, due to, as a result, since, for this reason, therefore, in order to, so that, thus . . .

Contrast: or, but, although, however, in contrast, nevertheless, on the other hand, while . . .

Addition or comparison: and, also, as well as, in addition, likewise, moreover, by the way . . .

Giving examples: for example, for instance, in particular, such as . . .

Polysemous Words Crisscross the Content Areas and the Tiers

We tend to think that words like *left, right, fall, table,* and *trunk* are easy Tier 1 words. However, due to their multiple meanings, these polysemous words can be very confusing to students in middle and high school when they hear *table* in a math or computer class, then hear *table* in a science class, and then are told to *table that discussion* in their social science class. Teachers can point out how the meaning of polysemous words such as these are to be used in their individual classrooms in comparison to other classrooms. More examples of easy-looking polysemous words are: *round, long, rest, roll, state, bank, face, leg, light, cell, power, check,* and *hand.*

A thought-provoking and fruitful Professional Learning Community (PLC) activity at the beginning of the year is teachers working in teams of four looking up all the meanings of easy words like those mentioned previously. They use their cell phones, iPads, or own experiences to list all the typical meanings, as well as collocations and idioms used in daily life at school and elsewhere. For example, *left* can be used in many ways, and some have very subtle differences indicated by the addition of one little word or two: the left side of a body, radical views, left field, past tense of leave, left out in left field, left in the dark, left behind, left for New York, left up to you, he left her, we left Maria out, left his post, left much to be desired, and past tense of "leave it at that." Another example is *leg.* Leg can be a limb, part of a table, stage of a journey, and a trouser leg. Leg can be used in idioms: no leg to stand on, break a leg, find one's leg, give someone a leg up, on one's last leg, and pull one's leg. After analyzing multiple meanings of polysemous words and phrases, teachers become sensitive to the proclivity for explaining their use in the immediate context. Some Tier 3 words, such as *power*, are used differently in the disciplines—for example, to the power of x (number) with the base meaning of multiplication, powerful speech, military power, party in power, power broker, electricity, power drive, horsepower, power lunch, power up, power down, power couple, and power behind the throne.

Preteach Vocabulary to Jumpstart Comprehension

Vocabulary instruction is most effective right at the beginning of a class—before any learning activity and before reading and writing. Teaching a word should take only two minutes—one minute for teacher presentation/explanation and one minute for peers to practice using it verbally.

Teachers have shied away from teaching vocabulary, particularly in middle and high schools, because many popular methods take up so much time. They have been asked to use strategies that take too much time, require content background knowledge, or are not evidence-based, such as the Frayer Model that calls for a student to fill in a quadrant with a definition, characteristics, examples, non-examples, and a picture. This leaves the vocabulary completely disconnected from the contextual meaning. In addition, ELs must comprehend each of the words used in the four quadrants for this to make sense to them. We have observed this method take up to 20 minutes with one word. Students are working individually on the quadrants, and then their work is stored in journals or binders, probably never to be seen again. A similar instructional model asks the students to first vote on a word to learn. Next, the teacher leads them in guessing what the word means. After several misguided guesses, they write or draw something to help remember the meaning. Finally, they write a sentence. This word becomes the word of the week. With this method, students will be explicitly taught *only* about 40 new words in a year. And again, these strategies are disconnected from the text. In addition to the long time it takes to work with one word, the biggest drawback is that students will never get close to learning the 3,500 to 5,000 words they need to learn in one year.

We tested these and other models for teaching vocabulary and compared student performance with each. Not finding good results, we decided to do our "components testing" of new strategies until we found the combination that worked for teachers and students. In that way, we came up with the 7-Steps process that takes only two minutes for students to learn a word. That implied that five words or phrases could be taught in 10 minutes at the beginning of each subject in elementary classrooms and at the beginning of each class period in middle and high schools for each content teacher to teach. When added up, students could learn 125 words per week, between 3,500 and 5,000 per year. The aforementioned crucial 3,500 to 5,000 words was reached when the polysemy of words was highlighted in each contextual meaning; when phrases were taught as chunks; when idioms or verb/noun clusters were taught together; and when, as appropriate, affixes, Greek and Latin roots, and compound words were taught and used in their contextual meanings in what students were about to read.

We then compared the 7-Steps process with the existing models and interviewed teachers and students and found this to be the most effective and efficient way to teach vocabulary.

Teaching Words and Phrases: 7 Steps for Preteaching Vocabulary

Words and phrases can be taught using the following steps:

1. The teacher asks students to repeat the word three times to practice pronunciation.
2. The teacher states the word and reads the sentence exactly as it is found in the text. (This allows students to remember its meaning within context from the text when they read it.)

3. The teacher provides the dictionary definition. (We don't want students to select the wrong meaning, and it takes up too much time for them to do it.)
4. The teacher provides a student-friendly definition or example to make sure that they understand the correct meaning.
5. The teacher highlights one feature: polysemous, cognate, tense, prefixes, and so on. If it is a polysemous word, additional meanings can be shared with students, but they must explicitly understand the contextual meaning used in this lesson/ text.

   Note: The following step (6) is the most important step.

6. Students pair up and, for one minute, give each other (Ping-Pong style) five or six examples of a vocabulary word in a teacher-provided sentence starter or frame that contains the word (e.g., target word: *polysemous*. "One example of a polysemous word is _____.").
7. The teacher holds students accountable for learning the word by informing them when to use it later on during partner summarization, in their exit pass, or in a writing assignment. (There is no student writing at this time; it adds too much time to the process. In Chapters 7 and 8, we provide examples of how students use the words during reading and writing.)

For Newcomers, a variation will suffice at the beginning: you can leave out Steps 3 (dictionary) and sometimes 5 (highlighting a grammatical feature) of the 7 Steps. Instead, give one or more examples of how to use the word to make sure they understand it well before they turn to their buddy to practice. For those who are working on pronunciation or whose curriculum focuses heavily on phonics in certain grades, the features-highlight step (the aforementioned Step 5 or the following Step 4) can be phonics related.

1. The teacher asks students to repeat the word three times to practice pronunciation.
2. The teacher states the word as found in the sentence in the text to help students remember its meaning within context from the text.
3. The teacher provides a student-friendly definition or examples to make sure that they understand the correct meaning.
4. The teacher highlights a phonics-related concept.
5. Students pair up and, for one minute, give each other (Ping-Pong style) five or six examples of a vocabulary word in a teacher-provided sentence starter or frame that contains the word (e.g., target word: *roars*. "A _____ roars.").

6. The teacher holds students accountable for learning the word and informs them when to use it later on during partner summarization, exit pass, or writing assignments. (Remember, no student writing at this time.)

The 7 Steps (or five or six steps for Newcomers/phonics instruction) are typically presented via PowerPoint. Students need to be able to see them as they process through them and refer to them in the student Ping-Pong step. In addition, teachers can save them and can upload to share with other teachers. The teacher uses one minute to teach Steps 1 through 5 when using the 7 Steps (or 1–3 or 4 when using the Newcomer/phonics-based variation). Step 6 (or 4 or 5 in the Newcomer/phonics variations) is used when students practice verbally in pairs and each uses a word in a sentence, five or six times in Ping-Pong style. For this flow, the teacher usually provides a sentence frame or a sentence starter containing the target word, thus ensuring that the word is used every time. This step (#6), when properly adhered to, provides the 12 productions/receptions of a word needed for students to start owning the words. These crucial 12 productions are the minimum needed for the brain to move the new vocabulary from short-term memory to long-term memory. The final step in each variation is only a few seconds to remind students when and how they will use or see the words.

We recommend teaching mainly Tier 2 words and phrases with the 7 Steps. For Tier 3 words, students need a lot of background knowledge to give various usage examples. They learn Tier 3 words when they read and study text features and do hands-on activities and other great activities during the course of the lesson. For example, students would be at a loss trying to use five or six examples of *osmosis* if that concept had not been introduced. They simply do not have the background to do so. We heard students attempt to use it by saying "Osmosis is good."; "We are studying osmosis."; and "I don't know examples of osmosis."

Instead, focus on Tier 2 words that surround a Tier 3 word or phrase to comprehend the concept. For example, the word *translation* is typically known in foreign-language classrooms. However, in math and science, its definition is nested in many Tier 2 words. In the examples that follow, Tier 2 words that help with comprehending the Tier 3 meaning of "translation" have been underlined. While these may not be the words Newcomers encounter, this example serves to illustrate the need to focus on Tier 2 words:

> **Translation** *is a term used in geometry to describe a function that moves an object a certain distance. The object is not <u>altered</u> in any other way. It is not <u>rotated,</u> <u>reflected,</u> or <u>resized</u>. In a translation, every point of the object must be moved <u>in the same direction</u> and for the same distance.*

> ***Translation*** *is the process of translating the sequence of a messenger RNA (mRNA) molecule to a sequence of amino acids during protein synthesis. The genetic code describes the <u>relationship</u> between the <u>sequence</u> of base pairs in a gene and the <u>corresponding</u> amino acid sequence that it encodes. (Note: the words* messenger *and* code *were not selected because, in this context, each is a part of a larger Tier 3 phrase,* messenger RNA *and* genetic code.*)*

For this reason, we do not want to send our students to the dictionary to look up definitions of Tier 3 words. First of all, if they are polysemous words, students will not know which definition to select. Instead, we focus on selecting the words that help define the Tier 3 words or phrases so that they can access their meanings in the context of reading the text, conducting and documenting experiments, and teacher-student discussions. In the previous example, the underlined words are the Tier 2 words and phrases that help define the polysemous term *translation*. There are other Tier 2 words that may need to be selected, and at times there will be too many to teach at one time, so use judicious scrutiny of the key vocabulary that will provide the most help to learn the content of that selection of text.

We also like to emphasize the benefit of selecting Tier 2 phrases, such as the following sentence starters, that are frequently used in class and can also be taught via the 7 Steps:

- This text is about _____.
- I liked the part where _____.
- I think this means _____.
- I don't understand the part about _____.
- That character reminds me of _____.
- That part reminds me of _____.
- This section is mostly about _____.
- The main idea is _____.
- The topic sentence is _____.
- Some details are _____.
- One argument might be _____.

Question starters, handy tools for Newcomers that can be taught via the 7 Steps, can sometimes be anticipated and planned for a lesson:

- Can you help me _____?
- I don't understand _____.
- Where is/are _____?

- How do I _____?
- May I ask a question?
- What does this word mean?
- How much time do we have for _____?
- Where do I _____?
- Would you please repeat that?
- Why is this different?
- What is the most important _____?

Assessing Vocabulary Acquisition

The ultimate proof that we want to see at the end of each class, each subject, and each week is how many words, phrases, and complete sentences students can write on an exit pass (a quarter or half a page) as an assessment of the content and language they learned. For example:

> *Write one or two paragraphs summarizing what you learned about _____ , using as many Tier 2 and Tier 3 words as you have learned. Use appropriate connectors, transition words, or signal words. Use compound sentences or different types of clauses.*

There is no need for vocabulary tests, such as matching definitions with words, since that is mainly a guessing game. Using the words in the proper context is the most efficient way of assessing their knowledge of vocabulary *and* content.

Evaluating Vocabulary Instruction Processes Schoolwide

Woodland Elementary is a school just starting to work on assessing their program of instruction for ELs. Here is an excerpt of what they came up with when they met to assess their students' vocabulary needs after a team of teachers attended a state-sponsored ExC-ELL Institute. This group of teachers formed Woodland's ExC-ELL PLC. Using one of our rubrics as a starter, the ExC-ELL PLC team assessed the school's current vocabulary instruction, contrasted with the ExC-ELL training they received. While working on their assessment, they rearranged our rubric to fit a similar one they use for other school improvement assessments (see Figure 6.5). They began with "Started" to give credit when due and as a base to begin assessing improvement. The team continued with "Needed," noting where the TLC felt the improvement process should start. In the last column, which they named "Success," they worked on "observable, measurable" items that they would be able to use in their end-of-year report as evidence of improvement and implementation and as a base for moving forward for the following year. In our opinion, they should use these as reasons to celebrate, too. (You'll see more of Woodland's self-assessment for reading and writing in Chapters 7 and 8.)

FIGURE 6.5 Rubric for Vocabulary Instruction to Help ELs Succeed in Content Areas

Vocabulary Acquisition

Process Component	Started (what we are doing now)	Needed (what else we need to do)	Success (evidence of improvement or implementation)
Which vocabulary Tier does our program focus on for instruction? What do we need to complement current instruction?	Most of our current vocabulary lists and the Words of the Day are Tier 3 words or phrases.	All our students need to know Tier 2 words that help understand contextual meaning of Tier 3 words. Obtain more instruction on selecting Tier 2 words and adding them to instruction.	Tier 2 words are posted in classrooms. All students are using Tier 2 words or phrases in context.
What is the source of our words selected for our vocabulary instruction?	The list is from our teachers' manuals.	Select Tier 2 words and phrases from our curricula's texts.	Tier 2 words are posted in classrooms. We are using Tier 2 words or phrases for the schoolwide Word of the Day program.
How are Newcomers introduced to new vocabulary?	We have no specific way. Sometimes we have them use a computer program.	Develop a Newcomer curriculum that includes needed survival and instructional vocabulary. Include critical Tier 1 words and phrases.	We are observing Newcomers and Level 1 ELs using correct vocabulary or responding appropriately when asked to participate during vocabulary instruction and later in reading and writing.

continued

FIGURE 6.5 **Rubric for Vocabulary Instruction to Help ELs Succeed in Content Areas** (continued)

Vocabulary Acquisition

Process Component	Started (what we are doing now)	Needed (what else we need to do)	Success (evidence of improvement or implementation)
How do Newcomers practice newly learned vocabulary?	Those who are able copy the words and definitions. Some teachers attended an ExC-ELL Institute and use sentence starters, preteach vocabulary, or scaffold.	Implement the 5 Steps for Preteaching Vocabulary to Newcomers. Provide models and time to practice new vocabulary.	Students are paired with higher-level ELs or native speakers and practice new vocabulary during instruction. Repeating what partners say is acceptable in the beginning.
How do we know Newcomers have acquired new target vocabulary?	We don't.	General content classroom teachers need to work with the ExC-ELL TLC.	We observe students practicing target vocabulary with partners during preteaching and later in reading and writing.
How do we enlist all our teachers to attend PD on the 7 Steps process?	ExC-ELL-trained teachers have invited colleagues to visit their classrooms to observe the 7 Steps.	All teachers will need to be trained in ExC-ELL.	We have implemented ExC-ELL vocabulary strategies schoolwide. Student tests and informal data will show increased vocabulary usage and improved test scores or advancement on WIDA's ACCESS and other tests.

Woodland Elementary Instruction for ELs and Newcomers: Overview and Next Steps, EL Vocabulary Instruction

At Woodland Elementary, we have vocabulary lists for each grade level and some whole-school target vocabulary as well. All teachers are required to highlight and include these works into each lesson where possible. The principal announces the Word of the Day and awards prizes when he hears them correctly used in classrooms or common areas. However, our newly formed ExC-ELL TLC has realized that most of these words are Tier 3 words or phrases, which means that our Newcomers, ELs, and striving learners may or may not fully understand them. Many times, they are not even related to the texts or lessons that students are engaging in. Therefore, we need to work on providing instruction and comprehension of Tier 2 words and phrases that help with Tier 3 comprehension—from what we expect our students to be reading. For our low-level ELs and Newcomers, we may need to provide instruction on Tier 1 words as well. This will mean our teachers and instructional staff will need training on how to (1) parse Tier 1, 2, and 3 vocabulary, (2) select the most critical to be taught, and (3) preteach them before students are expected to read. Ms. Puck, our principal, has agreed to work with a team to modify our Word of the Day program to feature cross-curricular, cross-grade-level, content-specific Tier 2 words and phrases. We know that we are well on our way when we see tiered vocabulary in place of word walls and when we review our data and see that all our students are using the correct contextual meaning of words in their classroom discussions and written assignments. We should also see improved reading, writing, and ACCESS scores at the end of the year.

Newcomers. We have very few Newcomers this year but have been informed that we will have a large number enrolled next year due to the local church providing resettlement assistance. For our current Newcomers, we have them use a popular computer-based language learning software and Mr. Quince, the ESL teacher, works with them for several hours each day. In addition, a few of our content teachers who have attended the state-sponsored ExC-ELL Institute are preteaching Tier 1 vocabulary, using sentence starters and other scaffolding. Going forward, for our Newcomers, teachers who will have the majority of Newcomers (one teacher from each grade level) will attend a Newcomer ExC-ELL training in addition to the ExC-ELL Institute. The Newcomer Teaching Team will work with Mr. Quince to develop a Newcomer curriculum inclusive of both survival and instructional Tier 1 English that supplements the instruction that they are receiving in their general and ESL classrooms. The Newcomer Teaching Team will make sure that they are implementing the 5 Steps for Preteaching Vocabulary to Newcomers, providing additional models, language buddies when possible, and lots of time to practice the target vocabulary. They will be able to document their success when Newcomers and Level 1 ELs are observed correctly using the target vocabulary, responding appropriately to the teacher's instructions, and using polite survival and instructional discourse in the classroom and later in reading and writing instruction and participation. The administration and coaching team will see higher-level ELs or native speakers working with the Newcomers as models. Depending on comfort level and ability, Newcomers may be repeating verbatim or partially repeating answers while working with partners. Day-one participation will always be the expectation. Success for students and teachers will be seen when Newcomers move to a higher ELD level and are more independent in their participation.

Whole school. Mr. Quince and the ExC-ELL-trained teachers have presented the 7 Steps for preteaching vocabulary at both a whole-staff meeting and again at grade-level meetings. They have invited and hosted teachers to watch the 7 Steps in action or to have them model the process in their classrooms. Ms. Puck and the leadership team have already planned the three-day ExC-ELL Institute for the beginning of next year and have communicated on several occasions that ExC-ELL is an expectation in all classrooms and subjects beginning no later than the start of next year. An ExC-ELL TLC has been formed, as well as a LIEP (Language Instruction Education Programs) Committee (formerly known as a LEP [Limited English Proficiency] Committee), and they facilitated this assessment and reviewed this action plan for compliance.

Summary

Vocabulary is the beginning; it is not an end in itself. Vocabulary taught in isolation from long lists has not proven to be effective. Without follow-up reading and writing, mastery of English vocabulary will be sparse and remain low level. Students need to use the target vocabulary in context while summarizing verbally what they just read or heard the teacher present. Afterward, they use it in writing to anchor language, literacy, and content knowledge. Chapters 7 and 8 pick up on that process.

7 Teaching Reading Comprehension

While researching ESSA requirements and the services other districts and states are providing, a member of the Newcomer/EL PLC team in Virginia came across a piece from the National Academies of Science, Engineering, and Medicine, "Conclusion 6-6: Evidence suggests that many schools are not providing adequate instruction to English learners (ELs) in acquiring English proficiency, as well as access to academic subjects at their grade level, from the time they first enter school until they reach the secondary grades" (2017, p. 266). You and your colleagues agree that this needs to be different at your school and wonder what strategies can be used to help the Newcomers access the curriculum through effective reading comprehension.

Reading from Day One

English learners need to read, discuss, and start writing to anchor new words just learned. For Newcomers in beginning stages, text should be broken into small segments. This way, while they are being successful with the shorter pieces of text, they are reading something different every day. Thus they are are engaged in greater analysis and application as they learn and apply new vocabulary, grammar, writing, and reading strategies. ELs and Newcomers accelerate their academic language learning when they read academic content books that are for beginning readers. On the other hand, simply repetitive reading of the same long passages does not help ELs and Newcomers develop fluency or comprehension since students tend to focus on "reading fast" or word calling and not on comprehension. Silent reading does not help, either; it becomes "pretend reading." Students can begin to think that skimming and looking at pictures is reading. These prevalent forms of reading only create ineffective habits that delay growth and depth of comprehension.

The following sequence of instruction engages Newcomers in reading by motivating interest in cognitive and conceptual strategies. The sequence covers all the necessary pieces that can be incorporated in either 90-, 60-, 30-, or 20-minute lessons. The sequence can go vertically, then continue horizontally the next day, as necessary. Fidelity to the sequence over the course of the year has shown statistically significant improvements in reading and academic discourse of Newcomers and other ELs in K–12.

Literacy is a multifaceted process that demands knowledge of the reading process, text structure, text features, and the author's purpose. For each facet of this process, we can teach key vocabulary to help ELs and other striving readers comprehend and learn what they read, as suggested in Chapter 6. While this preteaching of vocabulary is critical for all learners, it is especially critical for secondary-school-level Newcomers, who are required to read and learn from advanced, grade-level texts. Fortunately, Newcomers, other ELs, and striving readers do expedite their comprehension and learning when all teachers incorporate language and literacy instruction into their subject matter instruction. At another significant level, these students also need reengagement and full integration into grade-level classrooms; thus, peer interaction configurations proposed in this book undergird all learning.

Before students read a passage, the teacher prepares, models, and sets out tools, such as Table Tents with key phrases or words that the students can use during each phase of the reading process. The reading process begins with explicit instruction through modeling and student practice of text features, reading, summarizing, and ending with formulating their own questions to assess depth of comprehension and cooperative learning/debriefing as a class. With this process, students need to revisit the text several times and delve deeper into comprehension each time for different purposes and different skills development.

Phonological Awareness, Phonics, and Fluency

Literacy plays a pivotal role in helping Newcomers succeed in school and life. Upon their arrival at school, elementary-level Newcomers can begin their reading instruction along with oral language development in English. Children who are not taught to read by 3rd grade have difficulty learning academic content and academic discourse. Older Newcomers (those who arrive after 3rd grade) will need explicit instruction in English language phonics and fluency. Newcomers who learned to read in their first languages have reading skills and knowledge that they can draw on when learning to read in a second language with a little help on English phonics, spelling, and pronunciation.

Some Newcomers, however, come with interrupted formal education (that is, SIFE Newcomers) in upper elementary, middle, or even high school and might need basic reading skills typically developed in grades K–2. Depending on their level of reading development, they may be an emergent, beginning, or early instructional level readers. They will need guided instruction based on those levels to develop the characteristics related to reading, writing, and spelling. At the Emergent stage of reading development, they will need to develop an understanding of print and Concept of Word: correctly tracking words and spaces, syllables, and the direction of reading and writing. For those at the Beginning stage, they will need instruction on more than just decoding. At this stage, focus should be on beginning and ending sound awareness, differentiation between vowels and consonants, blends and diagraphs, and single-syllable words, of which many are Tier 1 words and eventually become automatically recognized. Those at the Early Instructional stage have a greater amount of sight words and understanding of vowel consonant patterns, have a beginning awareness of basic multisyllable words, and are at the Within Word Pattern stage. The Within Word Pattern stage, described by Bear, Invernizzi, Templeton, and Johnston (2016), is that stage where they are learning vowel patterns and sound layers with the result of being very creative in their spelling, such as *bot, bote, or bowt* for *boat*.

ESL and reading teachers can use a ready-made program for teaching phonics or beginning reading. In their review of programs for SIFE Newcomers, Geva and Ramírez (2015) found that Reading Instructional Goals for Older Readers (RIGOR) (Calderón, 2007) promotes literacy skills in both English and Spanish; the English version is being used with students from other language backgrounds as well.

RIGOR consists of a skill packet provided for each week of the year. Each skill bag contains a teacher's guide with daily lessons that include Tier 2 and Tier 3 words identified and laid out with the 7-Steps vocabulary instruction strategy described earlier, student books in hard copy and online, phonics activity cards, and weekly assessments that inform their learning progress. Interim tests provide progress reports. These lessons were tested in 17 schools in New York City, and 23 more schools have adopted the program. RIGOR was also tested with special education ELs in three schools. After two years, 95 percent of 8th graders who used the program were declassified as ELs and able to go on to general education classes in high school. This program supports the five Steps of an effective beginning literacy program for older readers in grades 5–12 using science and social studies books. The five components are:

1. Development of phonemic awareness and phonics skills
2. Development of vocabulary through the 7-Step instruction and practice sequences using Tier 2 (information-processing words) and Tier 3 words (subject-specific words)
3. Focus on reading comprehension, fluency, and content knowledge using science and social studies books
4. Use of writing to expand and reinforce literacy
5. Complete assessment data to inform instruction and move students to higher levels

Primary Language Reading

A study in dual-language schools found that Newcomers' learning was accelerated when they participated in English RIGOR in the morning and Spanish RIGOR in the afternoon. Using content-based or expository readers in the student's primary language accelerates learning to read in English. If the EL is sufficiently literate in their primary language, then reading to help comprehend the content in the student's primary language is a temporary support to jump-start learning English. There are a couple of reasons for this: (1) if they are reading about science, they learn the content and concepts and can muddle through the English text with more ease; and (2) math, science, and social studies disciplines contain over 40,000 cognates between English and Spanish. (Cognates are words that have almost the same sound, are spelled in virtually the same way—with no more than three letters that are dissimilar—and have the same meaning in two languages (e.g., president/presidente, photosynthesis/fotosíntesis, and factors/factores). However, this is a short-term strategy and teachers and students alike must avoid turning this into a translation crutch rather than a scaffold. Translation helps in many cases. Nevertheless, after a translation, the Newcomer must reiterate the concept in English. As soon as possible, instruction needs to be in English and production needs to be in English. The end-of-year tests are in English, aren't they?

Introducing the Lesson

Explaining the Lesson Objective or Standard

Teacher modeling always reflects the content standard and objective of the lesson. Even the brief description of an objective can be explained through a Think-Aloud. Following is an example:

Objective: Identify any statements or claims about climate change made by the author.

"I guess that means I have to find sentences or examples that say something about climate change. These can be called claims that the author makes about climate change. An author makes claims that can have scientific proof or not. I need to read the whole article to find if they have evidence or proof."

Explicitly Teach Text Features

Beginning with text features, teachers can use the Think-Aloud strategy to model how to use these tools to help Newcomers (and let's be honest, most other students) build a strong knowledge base of text features and text structures. From the text that students are about to read, the teacher selects a section to use to model text features—such as titles, captions, timelines, graphs, and even punctuation—and talks about their purposes. This metacognitive out-loud monologue-style discussion and analysis of the text helps students to explicitly see, decode, recode (comprehensible writing), and comprehend the text. For example (see Figure 7.1), in the diagram's text feature about the water cycle, this is what a Think-Aloud would sound like: *"Hmm, I see some words in the picture. Those must be the scientific words for what is happening in the water cycle. OK, let's see. There is a cloud with the word* condensation. *OK, that must be how clouds are made. Then there are water drops, but the label says* precipitation. *Oh, right, that's the scientific term for rain. There is an arrow going down. OK, rain falls and collects into lakes and oceans. Oh, wait,* collection *sounds like* collects. *I see a sun and another arrow going up. Hmm, I wonder if that means that the water is going up. The word is* evaporation. *I'll have to look for what that word means in the text."*

FIGURE 7.1 **Water Cycle**

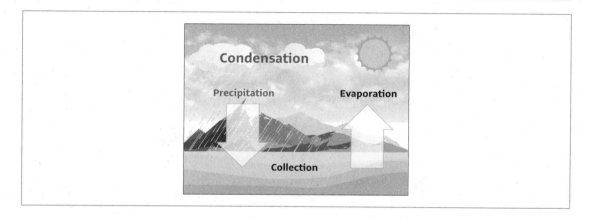

Teacher Think-Alouds help to teach students how to monitor their comprehension. When the text lends itself, the teacher can also model how to deconstruct a complex sentence to comprehend it or how to use other text features such as footnotes, bolding, or even punctuation such as quotation marks to help the reader navigate the text. Other times, a teacher can model how to go back to the beginning of a paragraph to find the cause for a particular effect. Think-Alouds can be turned into an assessment or individual student support (if the teacher asks the student to think out loud about what he is reading).

Student Tools

Students benefit from having tools on top of their desks or in their folders or journals. These can be Table Tents with examples of text structures or lists of words and phrases for cause and effect, other ways of saying *good*, or for asking questions.

For text features, you can create a chart explaining what each feature is and how it helps comprehension, such as the examples in Figure 7.2.

FIGURE 7.2 Nonfiction Text Features Charts

Text Feature	Purpose	Example
Photograph	Shows what something looks like (taken with a camera)	
Illustration	Shows what something looks like (drawn by an artist)	
Caption	Explains what a photograph or illustration is about	
Labels	Tell the names of certain parts of a photograph or illustration	
Graph	Organizes and helps compare information in a visual way	
Table	Organizes facts and numbers in a visual way so it is easier to read	

Text Feature	Purpose	Example
Title	Identifies the topic of the text/tells what the text will be about	
Title Page	Tells a book's title, author, illustrator, and publisher	
Table of Contents	Tells the names of the chapters and page the chapters can be found	
Index	Tells what page the reader can find certain topics	
Glossary	Tells the definition of some of the words found in the text	
Heading	Divides the text into section and explains what the section will be about	

Explicitly Teach Text Structures

The reading comprehension strategies that benefit native English speakers are the same strategies that Newcomers and other ELs need to develop: predicting, determining important information, summarizing, making inferences, visualizing, asking and answering questions, making connections, and monitoring comprehension. However, Newcomers and other ELs cannot be expected to make predictions or inferences if they do not understand a sufficient number of words in a passage or in the sentence starters or the discourse protocols for making and testing predictions. It is easier for Newcomers and ELs to begin practicing these strategies with a partner or buddy after they have been modeled by the teacher.

For remembering the differences between text structures, Newcomers need some tools. A simple one could be just for distinguishing the different structures and/or strategies that students are going to use. For example, a middle school teacher hands out charts like the one below. She instructs students to take notes as she explains the one that they need to use for this lesson. By the end of the semester, they have filled out all the spaces (as shown in Figure 7.3).

FIGURE 7.3 Reading Comprehension Strategies and Skills

Make note of the ones that your teacher wants you to use.

Predict	Persuade/argue
I think that his day will get better.	*I disagree. Alexander said that he wants to move, but . . .*
Determine important information	Make inferences
Her friend isn't talking to her. *She forgot her lunch money.* *She got an "F" on her quiz.*	*I'm guessing that . . .* *Based on what he said, that means . . .*
Ask and answer questions	Monitor comprehension
Why did Marc do that? *Susan stopped because . . .*	*I think that this means . . .*
Make connections	Summarize
This reminds me of . . .	*This paragraph is about how coal turns into diamond.*
Problem/solution	Describe/explain
The dog looked hungry, so she gave him her sandwich.	*In this part, Samuel . . . because . . . .* *For example . . .*

Simple charts, such as one outlining the differences between fiction and nonfiction, will help Newcomers begin to understand the author's craft and purpose. Examples are presented in Figure 7.4.

FIGURE 7.4 Differences Between Text Structures and Text Features

Fiction/Prose	Nonfiction/Expository/Informational
Made-up stories	Facts
Read in order (beginning, middle, ending)	Read in any order to focus on necessary information
Entertains readers	Teaches readers
Illustrations	Photographs
Some characteristics: • Plot • Characters • Setting • Conflict and solution • Point of view • Tone • Theme	Some characteristics: • Table of Contents • Glossary • Graphs and diagrams • Captions • Titles and subtitles • Sidebars • Bulleted lists

Additional examples of Table Tents can be found at ExC-ELL.com.

After Introducing the Lesson

Partner Reading and Summarizing

Now it is time for students to read. The teacher just modeled with a student how to do Partner Reading and now asks students to do the same:

Step 1. Read the first paragraph with your partner, alternating sentences. Partner A reads one sentence aloud, then Partner B reads the next sentence aloud. Use your soft voices.

Step 2. At the end of the paragraph, summarize the contents together. Try to use as many Tier 2 and Tier 3 words as you can.

Step 3. Read up to _____. We will have a discussion afterward.

Partner Reading needs to be accompanied by verbal summarization after each paragraph to display comprehension for self and for the teacher. Partner Reading works with the diversity of all student populations. It works if you have a class with only Newcomers, or mostly other ELs and a few Newcomers, or a general education classroom with only one or a handful of Newcomers. Advanced placement teachers use it because it quickly builds comprehension of complex texts. Whatever the population, the Newcomer should be partnered with a higher-ELD-level peer who can serve as a model. If all are Newcomers, working in pairs will still help tremendously. Just 10 minutes a day of daily reading in every subject expedites reading comprehension. Newcomers and other ELs need to hear themselves and others read for fluency and pronunciation. But, the main purpose is to go back into the text and analyze what they read so that they can summarize a paragraph verbally. They jointly practice their new language in a safe environment with peers. Partner Reading without Partner Summarization does not tell us if the Newcomer is comprehending. Note: For Partner Reading and Partner Summarizing, there is no writing at this time. All participation is oral.

Partner Reading and Partner Summarizing (orally) engages all students in reading at the same time with 100 percent participation. With other strategies such as Round Robin, ELs typically get to read only one or two sentences. They are often left out when a teacher calls on individual students in a core-content class or are too timid to volunteer. Silent Reading is a waste of precious instructional time and not well-suited for ELs. One never knows if they are comprehending when reading silently.

Triad Reading with Newcomers

When we train for Partner Reading, we also train teachers for Triad Reading. All our schools use the following strategy for Newcomers, as Triad Reading is more effective. This is where a Newcomer sits in the middle of students A and B. As A reads a sentence, the Newcomer whisper-reads along with A. When B reads the next sentence, the Newcomer whisper-reads along with B. After two or so weeks of daily Partner Reading in different subjects, the Newcomer will be ready to take a turn. The reading sequence will then be: A reads, Newcomer reads, B reads, Newcomer reads. That means that the Newcomer gets double turns, thereby accelerating her reading improvement. They also have the benefit of support from their reading partners.

Triad Summarizing with Newcomers

The pattern from Triad Reading is also used for the Triad Summarization. At first, the Newcomer listens and repeats what students A and B are saying as they summarize. After a couple of weeks, they add to the summary by using short phrases or sentences.

After all, you have pretaught vocabulary for that section, and the Newcomer has read with two partners. That means that she has picked up a few phrases and has comprehended sufficiently to be able to add to the summary (which she's ready to do as you've already practiced some sentence or summary starters). Again, no writing at this time.

After Reading and Summarizing: Debriefing and Discussion

While students are reading and summarizing out loud with their reading buddies, the teacher moves around the room and records individual progress and successes. As the teacher listens, he can also record some words that need further clarification or concepts that need attention. After students complete their partner reading, here are some ways to debrief with the whole class about their own performance, their thinking, and additional unknown words or concepts that the teacher overheard:

- Students are asked to report on words and phrases they didn't understand. (One strategy is to have students list unknown words on Post-it notes, and then the teacher picks them up as they move around the room monitoring the summaries.)
- The teacher offers clarification of unknown words/phrases.
- A student from each team reports on the gist of one paragraph.
- The teacher facilitates the clarification of overall meaning of the paragraph (then on larger chunks, as appropriate).
- The teacher poses a question for students to reflect and discuss, such as, "How does this relate to what you've learned before?"

After Reading and Summarizing, Time for Writing Text-Dependent Questions: How to Anchor Knowledge, Language, and Literacy

The next step is for the partners (pairs of students) to sit in teams of four and practice formulating questions on the passages they read and summarized verbally. Each team of four writes one or two questions on an index card and the answer on the back of the card. They can also give themselves a team name to create a sense of unity as they work together on this task.

To generate quality questions, a teacher needs to model how to write questions, and the different varieties of questions, even those known as prompts or those that do not end with a question mark. Using a taxonomy such as Bloom's, the Newcomers can begin at Level-1 type questions and gradually move toward the HOTS (higher order thinking skills) style questions throughout the year. These questions help Newcomers pay attention to specific words, details, and concepts. As peers discuss choices in their team, Newcomers also pick up on procedural learning and collaborative skills. Writing questions helps all students delve deeper into the text. This is what we mean by "close reading"; yet another reentry into the text to help with solidifying content mastery. Writing questions gets students back into the text to find new pieces of information, claims, counterclaims, citations, connections with other text features, or to simply consolidate language, literacy, and content.

After the teams have written their questions, the teacher collects them, checks them, and then uses them to assess the entire class' comprehension and text-based discourse. Typically, teachers use the Cooperative Learning strategy Numbered Heads Together, which has been around since the 1970s. We have modified it a bit to use as a follow-up to the question formulation activity. The teacher posts (and explains and models the activity with one team) a slide with instructions. See the following script/instruction slide, and be sure to read and summarize the instructions with your students.

NUMBERED HEADS TOGETHER

1. Number off in your team from one to four.
2. Listen to the question.
3. Put your heads together and find the answer. You only have two minutes.
4. Make sure everyone in your team knows the answer, assisting team members as needed.
5. Be prepared to answer when I call your number.
6. The team that wrote the question will be the language monitors or coaches. It is your role to write down sentence starters, connectors/transitions, Tier 2, and Tier 3 words used by the students I call on. (Use our Respectful Discourse Table Tents.)

These steps for developing reading comprehension ensure success for Newcomers. They have prepared by learning five words at the beginning, learning more Tier 2 and 3 words and phrases during Partner Reading, putting discourse together and practicing it during Partner Summarization, participating in close reading, and formulating questions. During the two minutes that teams discuss the answers to a question another team wrote, peers help Newcomers and other ELs learn a brief, correct response that they can use in case their number is called. Responding correctly enhances self-confidence and self-esteem. It motivates the Newcomer to keep responding and improving. It also teaches other students empathy, respect for difference, and cooperative skills.

Most important, due to the redundancy of these steps in reading and reentering the text, students master the content. This is critical for middle and high school students. Instead of attempting to read long chapters on their own, all students benefit from the set of interactive instructional events (entering and reentering the text), from which they learn to process information. The socioemotional and cognitive skills learned will transfer into other learning experiences. The set of reading components works best when teachers parse the text and select only sections that teach the necessary key concepts. Often, textbooks and online texts have some superfluous information. This consumes too much time in class when it comes to discussions or calls for an extra day to reteach everything. We have also observed how students enjoy and learn more content in advanced placement classrooms when teachers employ all these reading phases.

How to Connect More Word Knowledge During the Reading Process

During the reading activity sequence, students are being exposed to more words. A few words will be learned in the context of reading. Other words need to be explicitly taught. Most will be learned on the run as students interact with others to complete their tasks. Below are three examples of activities that help Newcomers learn more vocabulary and discourse.

Vocabulary Roundtable Review of Tier 2 and 3 Words and Phrases

After Numbered Heads Together, the students can stay in teams of three or four for the Vocabulary Roundtable review. More than four students in a team is too many to sustain engagement. The objective is to write down on one sheet of paper that circulates around the table from student to student within each team as many Tier 2 and 3 words as they can remember that they learned from the reading section. The Roundtable has three parts that are introduced one at a time. The instructions for the Vocabulary Roundtable are as follows (noting that we've provided the script for the instructions, which can be posted or displayed via PowerPoint):

PART 1—SET UP

- Clear your desks.
- Only one sheet of paper per team is needed, but everyone needs a pencil.

- Each student will write one key Tier 2 or Tier 3 word or phrase and then pass the paper to the right. Everyone must write a word or phrase.
- When I say "start," continue until I call time.

ROUND 1—ACTION

- Write a Tier 2 or Tier 3 word or phrase from the text and pass the paper to the right.
- Keep writing one word or phrase at a time until the teacher calls "stop." You have one minute.
- The words and phrases must be Tier 2 or 3.

ROUND 1 (CONT.)—CHECK AND COUNT

- Eliminate repeated words.
- Count the correct words your team wrote.
- Write the total at the top of the page and be ready to tell the teacher your team's total.

PART 2—STRATEGIZE

- Let's do it again. Put your heads together and come up with a strategy to improve your team total.
- Reread/revisit the text.
- Learn more words.
- You have three minutes.

PART 3—ROUND 2

- Apply your strategy to Round 2.
- Follow the same rules as for Round 1.
- Let's see how much you improve the second time.

Who improved? The answer is usually everyone! When debriefing, students recognize that with a little more effort they can surpass their initial attempt. They also learn which strategies work toward improvement and which should be avoided. Additionally, team collaboration improves as they encounter new challenges.

Defining Words During Reading

Even after teachers preteach five keywords to help students enter into reading, the students will still need to learn more words as they read. As teachers monitor Partner Reading, they will soon become aware of these words. They should monitor with notebook, tablet, or laptop in hand to record the words or items that need teaching during reading. Teaching on the run occurs after students finish reading and summarizing a paragraph with their partner, when teachers can pause and quickly give examples of the words they found problematic and how they are being used in the text. Teachers should refrain from correcting pronunciation when students are reading or summarizing. Redirection (pronunciation or other corrections) can be done during debriefing, similar to Step 1 of the 7 Steps, without naming names. Just have students repeat after you, three times, words that are difficult to pronounce.

Highlighting Prefixes, Root Words, and Suffixes

At times, depth of word knowledge can be taught "on the run" by highlighting affixes and/or root words. These word modifiers can also be given to students after an explanation of how they work:

- -able, -ible (can be done)
- -er, -or (person)
- -er (comparative)
- -est (comparative)
- -tion, -ion, -ation, -ition (act, process)
- -en (made of)
- -ed (past-tense verbs)
- -ing (present participle)
- -s, -es, (plural)
- -ly (characteristic of)
- -y (characterized by)
- -ity, -ty (state of)
- -ive, -ative, -itive (adjective form of a noun)
- -less (state of)
- -ous, -eous, -ious (possessing the qualities of)

Sentence Structures

Pointing out sentence types in text also makes grammatical structures easier to understand and remember. Sentence structures are another great Think-Aloud item to metacognitively highlight. Using a grammar book or grammar program, typically not connected to the text students are reading, as a device to teach grammar or sentence structure usually does not help Newcomers because these do not provide sufficient in-context usage. However, when students encounter a complex sentence during reading and have to muddle through to understand and learn the content, it makes better sense, and they remember it longer. Simple sentence structures (subject-verb-object) can be taught before writing. If there is a complex sentence, that becomes a great opportunity to show how its parts fit together. One structure you want to highlight is how connectors or transition words (however, but, or, nevertheless, additionally, so) help connect facts, ideas, or thoughts. Write the sentence on the SMART Board and show what the connector is indicating (i.e., Honolulu is a fabulous island; *however,* I prefer Kauai. I prefer Kauai *but* don't go very often. My friend was going to Honolulu, *so* I went with him). Processing these structures while reading, using real-life text examples, will help students to be able to use them in their own writing later.

Self-Efficacy

Most Newcomers arrive with built-in strengths to overcome struggles and barriers. As educators, we can tap into these intrinsic resources to help them sustain their efforts in a new setting. Unfortunately, teachers often either overprotect them or end up ignoring them because they don't know what to do with them. The effort a Newcomer puts forward is sometimes misunderstood because they apply what has worked in the past, which is culturally and experientially different. Nevertheless, teachers can guide their choices and perseverance by keeping Newcomers engaged in an active reading/learning process. Providing opportunities for genuine competency and a sense of self-accomplishment is a strong way to boost their self-esteem (Bandura, 1985). We must constantly seek "the right rigor" for Newcomers and other ELs.

We can turn their mistakes into learning opportunities when we debrief with them, their teams, or the whole class. Instead of praising all the time, we can ask, "What did you learn from this? What will you do differently next time?" Reflection questions such as these help to build and sustain a growth mindset. This is why instructional events such as two rounds of Vocabulary Roundtable were strategically designed. The three-minute interval between the first and second try is for students to ponder and pursue strategies for improvement.

In a Nutshell

In essence, reading comprehension in any content area or ESL/ELD classroom entails several phases that build on each other. When one is skipped, the others suffer. We should not ask Newcomers, LTELs, or any striving reader to jump into comprehension (or close reading, as it is called these days) without vocabulary instruction and practice as it is described in this chapter. The benefits are quickly evident. Teachers usually start by doing all the phases with one class in secondary schools, or one small group of students, or one subject in elementary school. To their amazement, they quickly see the benefits and apply the process with other groups. The following tips have been collected from the Virginia school districts with which we've been working and which succinctly lay out the heart of ExC-ELL reading comprehension.

Following is a brief recap of the reading stages and strategies outlined in this chapter:

- Math, science, social studies, and literature are best learned though a multi-faceted reading process and explicit vocabulary instruction.
- Parse the text into small, manageable sections in which new vocabulary needs to be introduced.
- Teach five words from the texts that students are about to read in each subject area.
- Focus on Tier 2 words before they enter the text. Tier 3 words are learned from reading how the texts define them and from close reading activities.
- Model reading comprehension strategies through brief Think-Alouds.
- Text Features help comprehension.
- Explicitly connect Text Structure with content and language objectives.
- Peer interaction throughout all these reading phases develops oracy and comprehension.
- Cooperative Learning in teams of four fosters positive socioemotional skills as well as depth of comprehension and discourse.
- Strategic use of student tools, such as Table Tents with sentence frames, question starters, and cognitive maps help all learners.

Evaluating Reading Comprehension Processes Schoolwide

As we learned at the end of Chapter 6, Woodland Elementary was just starting to work on assessing their program of instruction for ELs. Here is an excerpt from what they came up with when they met to assess their students' reading comprehension and instruction needs after a team of teachers attended a state-sponsored ExC-ELL Institute. This group of teachers became part of the newly formed ExC-ELL PLC and invited Ms. Oberon, the reading specialist who is working on her ESOL certification. They modified the same rubric for their Vocabulary Instruction review for this Reading Comprehension assessment rubric. As with other Woodland School improvement assessments, they began with the "Started" column to give credit when due and as a base to begin assessing improvement (see Figure 7.5). The team then used the "Needed" column for notes on where the ExC-ELL TLC felt the improvement process should start. In the last column, which they named "Success," they worked on observable, measurable items that they would be able to use in their end-of-year report as evidence of improvement, implementation, and as a basis for moving forward for the following year. Even more to celebrate! Look for the Vocabulary Instruction assessment in Chapter 6 and follow up in Chapter 8 with the Writing Instruction and Putting It All Together assessment rubiric.

FIGURE 7.5 Rubric for Instructional Strategies to Help ELs Succeed in Reading Comprehension in Content Areas

---

Reading Comprehension

Process Component	Started (what we are doing now)	Needed (what else we need to do)	Success (evidence of improvement or implementation)
What prereading strategies do we explicitly teach? • Text Features? • Text Structures? • Objectives?	We post standards and read them to students. Most classrooms have Text Features posters. Most classrooms have Text Structure/ Author's Craft posters.	Post language objectives and help students understand expectations. Obtain more explicit instruction on Text Features and Text Structures.	Students summarizing objectives and expectations with partners. In student Cooperative Learning activities, students correctly identify Text Features or author's purpose/ Text Structure

continued

FIGURE 7.5 Rubric for Instructional Strategies to Help ELs Succeed in Reading Comprehension in Content Areas (*continued*)

Reading Comprehension

Process Component	Started (what we are doing now)	Needed (what else we need to do)	Success (evidence of improvement or implementation)
What comprehension concepts or strategies do we teach/model?	We have students do Reading Guides.	Model Think-Alouds: Text Features, Text Structure, or Fix-It strategies. Implement and model Partner Reading and Partner Summarization. Implement and model text-based Question Formulation. Implement and model discourse protocols for summarizing to facilitate Close Reading.	When summarizing with partners, students use modeled Think-Alouds to process text. We achieved 100 percent participation in Partner Reading and Partner Summarization. In student Cooperative Learning activities, students correctly formulate text-based questions and answers. Students revisit text or use discourse strategies.
What does reading look and sound like in our classrooms?	We use Sustained Silent Reading, teacher read-aloud, Popcorn Reading, and Reader's Theater. For higher-level students, some teachers have students read silently and then discuss in pairs what they read at the end of the reading time.	Implement Partner Reading and Partner Summarization in all contents. Implement Partner Summarization after Partner Reading and Paired Silent Reading, with Partner Summarization after each page or section. Have students revisit text when they do not agree.	Students will be reading aloud in quiet voices in pairs and summarizing. Students will be alternating reading aloud sentences, then summarizing at the end of each paragraph. All students will use polite discourse protocols to summarize and agree or disagree with reading buddies.

Process Component	Started (what we are doing now)	Needed (what else we need to do)	Success (evidence of improvement or implementation)
When are Newcomers expected to read?	Newcomers are allowed to wait until they are comfortable reading.	Implement and model Newcomer Triad Reading and Summarizing.	Newcomers are teamed with higher-level ELs or native speakers and participate in Partner Reading and Triad Partner Summarization at various levels: • Whisper Reading • Repeating sentences • Reading own sentences with partner support.
What tools and support do Newcomers need to use for reading and comprehension?	They have language buddies who speak the same language and can interpret. They have class with the ESL teacher.	Develop and use in all subjects: • Table Tents • Sentence Starters • Word Banks Develop a Newcomer curriculum based on basic reading skills, Concept of Word, and phonics. (See Figure 6.5 vocabulary instruction rubric.)	Table Tents and other supports are available and being used by students when observed. We have observed reading strategy instruction targeted at Newcomers. We use Newcomer Triads to allow all students to participate.
How do we know Newcomers are comprehending what they read? What data are we collecting?	They get translated quizzes from the ESL teacher, but we have some languages that the ESL teacher doesn't speak. End-of-year test scores reflect comprehension and serve as data.	Collect data from Partner Reading, Partner Summarization, and Triad Reading and Summarizing. Implement (and collect data from) Cooperative Learning activities, such as text-based question formulation, Numbered Heads Together, use of Tier 2 and Tier 3 vocabulary (Tier 1 for Newcomers), and writing samples. (See Figure 8.6 writing rubric.)	Data shows mastery of content and usage of comprehension skills, Tier vocabulary, and polite discourse. Students collaboratively learn in teams.

continued

FIGURE 7.5 **Rubric for Instructional Strategies to Help ELs Succeed in Reading Comprehension in Content Areas** (*continued*)

Reading Comprehension

Process Component	Started (what we are doing now)	Needed (what else we need to do)	Success (evidence of improvement or implementation)
How many teachers will we need to train in the recommended reading components of this book?	Almost all; one ESL teacher went to the state-sponsored introductory session.	Obtain PD for general classroom teachers in reading strategies for Newcomers and other ELs.	We achieved whole-school implementation of ExC-ELL and improvement of student test scores and informal data.

Woodland Elementary Instruction for Newcomers and Other ELs: Overview, Next Steps, and EL Reading Comprehension Rubric

At Woodland Elementary, we have worked hard to create classroom posters to help students understand the standards and expectations of reading. Ms. Oberon, our reading specialist, has worked with the teachers so that most classrooms have posters identifying Text Features, such as bold, italicized, or highlighted words and others like titles, subheadings, captions, and diagrams. Other posters have examples of Author's Craft or Text Structures—such as theme, point of view, and signal words—for comparing and contrasting, identifying problems and solutions, and other similar structures. Teachers post standards and objectives along with Essential Questions for each lesson in the same place every day and students copy them to their Learning Logs each day after summarizing and discussing them with their reading buddies. We also use the Reading Guides from our curriculum and student workbooks and have created our own Reading Guides for those curricula that haven't provided them.

After reviewing the Reading Comprehension session and strategies from the ExC-ELL Institute, we will be adding Language Objectives to complement the Content Objectives and to help our ELs understand how they will use English to show mastery of the content. The ExC-ELL PLC teachers have already started this, along with an oral review and student summary of both types of objectives. When feasible, teachers refer to the objectives to remind all students of the expectations. One teacher has also found that reviewing the objectives at the end of the lesson to be an effective assessment of how far students made it through her lesson and makes notes on where to pick it up for the next time. This strategy will be added to the implementation plan. The ExC-ELL TLC team will develop and provide examples of how to do Think-Alouds from the mentor texts based upon Text Features and Text Structures that will fit our current pacing guide and lesson structure.

For our reading time and instruction, we currently use SSR, teacher read-aloud, Popcorn Reading, and Reader's Theater. Ms. Oberon also has a few pull-out groups for those students who are one or more grade levels below where they need to be.

We will roll out Partner Reading and Partner Summarization by modeling and practicing in our grade-level meeting and will introduce them as soon as possible, no later than the beginning of next year. Our higher-level students will start with the Partner Reading and Partner Summarization basics and should be able to progress to other high-level variations quickly. All students will also receive Table Tents, teacher Think-Aloud demos, and modeling of appropriate discourse for summarizing. We will explicitly model how to reenter the text for clarification when students do not agree with one another in their summarizing or other discussions.

Many classrooms use Reciprocal Teaching and Socratic Seminars, among other Cooperative Learning activities. For greater depth of content mastery, by the end of October of next school year, we will have introduced content-based question formulation to our students, after practicing and planning in our grade-level meetings. This will require mini-lessons on Bloom's Taxonomy and how to formulate open-ended questions. By the end of November, we will roll out Numbered Heads Together as a Cooperative Learning strategy. Several teachers currently do a variation of this and will start sooner.

Our Leadership Team and others will be able to see evidence of strategy implementation during their Learning Walks. By using the WISEcard, they will be able to make note of students summarizing objectives and instructions. Observers of students working with reading buddies on Partner Reading and Partner Summarization will hear students reading and summarizing using Tier 2 and 3 vocabulary during buddy reading. Teams of three to four students will be creating Bloom's-level questions based on the text, and later they will have classroom debriefing in which they use their questions to quiz classmates. The target is 100 percent participation in all activities, even for low-level ELs or

Newcomers. All student-student and student-teacher interactions and discussions will be facilitated with appropriate discourse as modeled, practiced, and shown on classroom posters or Table Tents.

Newcomers. Currently, Newcomers are paired with language buddies when available and allowed to participate when they feel comfortable. To bolster their comfort level while setting the expectation that all students, including Newcomers, are expected to participate each day, the Newcomer Teaching Team is currently working on the Newcomer curriculum basics for reading, which will include phonics, letter-sound recognition, Concept of Word, text recognition, and sentence structure and mechanics. The Newcomer and ESL teachers will model participation strategies such as repeating what classmates have said, choral repetition of pretaught vocabulary, whisper reading in Triad Reading and Summarizing, and asking for assistance when needed. Mr. Quince, the ESL teacher, will work with our Newcomers on survival and instructional language as well as helping to provide sentence starters, Table Tents, and other supports.

Newcomers currently receive translated quizzes when possible. However, with the implementation of ExC-ELL strategies, students will be able to comprehend and practice necessary content specifics enough to be able to participate in the same quizzes and assessments as their peers. Modifications will be provided as required by the LIEP plan or for any dually identified student with an Individual Education Program (IEP). In addition, informal data will serve as evidence of mastery and will be gathered on all students when participating in Partner Reading, Partner Summarization, Numbered Heads Together, and the other Cooperative Learning activities already in place. Writing samples will also provide a portfolio of evidence of mastery and usage.

Observers and the administration team will see Newcomers participating with their peers and will see growth at the end of the year on the WIDA ACCESS 2.0 tests and other end-of-year assessments.

Whole-School. Mr. Quince and the ExC-ELL-trained teachers have presented Partner Reading, Partner Summarization, and Numbered Heads Together at a whole-staff meeting and again at grade-level meetings. They have invited and hosted teachers to watch these reading comprehension strategies in action or have offered to model them in their classroom. Ms. Puck and the Leadership Team have already planned the three-day ExC-ELL Institute for the beginning of next year and have highlighted that reading comprehension is a large, districtwide initiative for next year and that Woodland Elementary will be the pilot school for ExC-ELL—thus it is an expectation in all classrooms and subjects beginning no later than the start of next year. The ExC-ELL TLC facilitated this assessment and the Vocabulary and Writing Instruction rubrics and will be working with the LIEP Committee to review this action plan for compliance.

8 Teaching Writing

"*The six golden rules of writing: read, read, read, and write, write, write.*"

—Ernest Gaines, Author

As college graduates, we have used writing to learn and prove what we have read and learned. "The importance of writing to learn helps students develop the habit of writing, to understand writing as a representation of what they think, and to use writing to foster further, deeper thinking and to integrate knowledge" (Carroll & Wilson, 2008, p. 326).

While planning lessons, you and your colleagues have realized that in your Teacher Learning Communities (TLC) you need to work with each other to share strategies, ideas, and writing success stories. You might also be required to show how your lessons are rigorous and relevant. It takes practice to balance your content with rigor and strategies so that all learn. "Teachers in all disciplines and on all levels come to grips with a definition of writing that includes thought and learning. When we do, we will be better equipped to incorporate writing to maximize learning and enhance the intellectual rigor of students" (Carroll & Wilson, 2008, p. 327).

Teaching Writing to Newcomers and Striving Writers

The final piece in the instruction sequence suggested in ExC-ELL (items 10–12 in Figure 6.1) is writing about what is being learned. We can call this text-based writing. Small pieces of writing related to what ELs are reading can be introduced daily, with one summative piece each week or at the end of each unit.

Grammatical/syntactical features—such as prepositional phrases, spelling, tense, compound sentences, and passive voice—are understood and applied in student writing quicker when the teacher points out these features from the Mentor Text that the students have read.

Writing in science is different from writing about historical events and formulating mathematical questions. All content writing is definitely different from the writing process most students have been exposed to in language arts. Hence, it behooves every teacher in the school to revisit writing via professional development on teaching writing in the subject areas.

Just as in reading, teaching writing consists of several phases of explicit instruction—modeling, practice with peers, and feedback through debriefing. The features and phases of writing instruction are based on research about writing by Graham and Hebert (2010) but modified for Newcomers and other ELs (Calderón & Slakk, 2018):

1. *Preteach the most important vocabulary.* Select key words that students will need to understand and use for writing assignments and grading.
2. *Use a Mentor Text for reading before writing.* Reading a text gives students the content and sample sentence structures to use in their writing. This is why we call it a Mentor Text. Mentor Texts develop background knowledge or explanations of unfamiliar concepts and mechanics for writing.
3. *Present the text structure to use.* Discuss and present the structure (e.g., argumentative, descriptive, or narrative) and its purpose, benefits, and goals, as well as the grading rules of finished products.
4. *Model it.* Model each phase of the writing process (e.g., drafting in teams, revising, editing, and final product).
5. *Memorize it.* Ensure that students memorize the language and steps of the strategy.
6. *Support it.* Support or scaffold ELs' use of the strategy until they can apply it with little or no support. Model self-regulated learning and the use of mnemonic devices.

7. *Ample use of student interaction.* Model and implement collaborative and cooperative writing strategies to plan, draft, revise, and edit compositions.
8. *Differentiated assessment.* Consider differentiated grading scales for ELs, depending on their level of English proficiency. Assess the point of entry for writing and continue measuring the learning progression of writing, since the oral, reading, and writing proficiencies for ELs vary dramatically. A Newcomer may have good writing skills in his primary language, but writing styles and standards from the Newcomer's home country may be different from our expectations. A student who has been in U.S. schools since kindergarten may have oral fluency but no literacy skills in either the first or second language (Calderón, 2011 a; 2011b).

Short Pieces of Writing

Exit passes and short summaries serve as both a quick assessment and the accountability piece you indicated students would be held to in Step 7 of the 7 Steps of Preteaching Vocabulary, but remember that this is not a written part of Step 7 and that this accountability comes later in the lesson (see Chapter 6).

Initially, teachers ask ELs to write individual summaries or a couple of sentences on an exit pass on their own or in pairs. After teachers model various strategies to revise and edit writing, the students apply the strategies in pairs or teams. This collaboration helps them to clarify and learn more about writing. This is also the time to teach more vocabulary to students. They will need more connectors, transition words, and words for elaborating their sentences. Subsequently, they begin writing longer summaries, compositions, and reports. Their Table Tents are always in full view as reminders.

Keep in mind that after going through the majority of the 12 components, the students have used the five or six pretaught words at least 40 times, and now they own them. There is no reason to doubt that they can write using that vocabulary. If the teacher has monitored and heard them using these words in their Partner Reading and Summarization pairs, seen them use them when they formulated questions, heard them use these words when they answered questions during Numbered Heads Together and did various types of writing during all the follow-up activities, then there is no reason to reteach any of those words or phrases. The students have mastered them. They know text-based content, words, and sentence structures because they have seen them, used them, and heard/discussed them with their peers.

Cooperative Learning Strategies Embedded in the 12 Components

Note that for every component included so far, structured Cooperative Learning methods support and consolidate each step toward comprehension. In cooperative activities, learners are accountable for their own learning and for that of their teammates. Working with peers is beneficial for all K–12 ELs and even their non-EL peers as they learn to apply English literacy and content learning in the classroom. You will soon notice that the greatest benefit to this type of learning for Newcomers and other ELs is that it builds confidence for self-expression as they practice articulating their thoughts in the safety of their teams, particularly before whole-class discussions. As confidence grows, so does language, literacy, and content mastery.

Cooperative Learning is used during:

- Step 6 of the 7 Steps for Preteaching Vocabulary
- Partner Reading and Partner Summarization
- Question Formulation
- Numbered Heads Together to assess content comprehension and discourse acquisition
- Writing during drafting
- Writing during revising
- Writing during editing
- Team building, summarizing in teams, reviewing in teams, and team products.

It is extremely important that the whole cycle of vocabulary, reading, and writing (see Figure 8.1) be completed. It may take approximately 90 minutes or two 45-minute class periods, or a combination thereof after students and the teacher become proficient with the strategies. The first few times, it will take longer as each strategy and piece is introduced, practiced, and refined. After studying the cycle, we learned that teaching vocabulary yields only 30 percent of student growth. Adding all the reading components to vocabulary instruction yields about 65 percent of growth. Ultimately, adding writing components to vocabulary and reading yields 90 to 100 percent of the instructional goals that are expected in the individual teacher's objectives.

FIGURE 8.1 Cycle of Comprehension

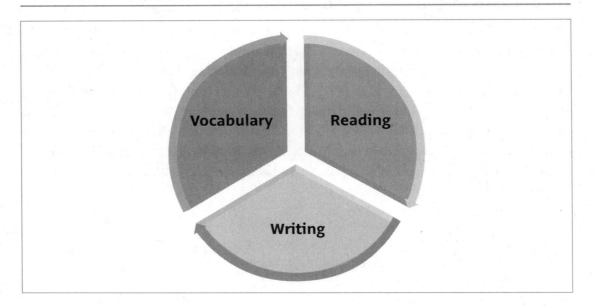

Types of Writing/Writing Genre

Writing standards are grounded in evidence from either literary or informational texts. State standards typically call for the following percentages of time and assessments while teaching writing:

- Elementary school: 30 percent to argumentative, 35 percent to explain/inform, and 35 percent narrative
- Middle school: 35 percent to argumentative, 35 percent to explain/inform, and 30 percent narrative
- High school: 40 percent to argumentative, 40 percent to explain/inform, and 20 percent narrative

Students need to demonstrate their knowledge through precision and detail in various types of writing: historical, technical, and scientific. Accuracy matters!

College and career-readiness standards describe these types of writing as text types, text structures, or writing structures. The standards also give the purpose for writing through these text types, as illustrated in Figures 8.2, 8.3, and 8.4.

FIGURE 8.2 State Writing Standards for College and Career Readiness

Text Type	Purpose
Arguments	To change the reader's thinking, move the reader to action, or convince the reader to accept the writer's explanation of a problem or concept by supporting claims with clear reasons and relevant evidence.
Informative/Explanatory	To examine a topic and convey ideas, concepts, and information through the selection, organization, and analysis of relevant content to increase knowledge, explain a procedure, or explore a concept in depth.
Narratives	To entertain, instruct, or inform by developing real or imagined experiences or events using effective techniques, relevant descriptive details, and well-structured event sequences.

Source: www.bcps.org/offices/lis/writing/secondary/types.html#narrative

FIGURE 8.3 Typical State Standards for Writing Type Prompts: Key Words

Argumentative	Informative/ Explanatory	Narrative
To what extent	Analyze	Describe
Defend	Explain	Identify
Pros and cons	Examine	Outline
Take a stand	Evaluate	Show

FIGURE 8.4 Writing Structure and Purpose: State Standards for Writing to Learn

Writing Structure	Purpose
Problem/Solution	Show the development of a problem and one or more solutions to the problem. The author states a problem and various solutions or uses a question-answer format and addresses the problem.
Compare/Contrast	Point out likenesses and/or differences among facts, people, events, or concepts.
Cause/Effect	Show how facts, events, or concepts happen or come into being because of other facts, events, or concepts.
Description	Address a specific topic and its attributes. Provide main idea(s) supported by rich/descriptive details.
Sequence	Provide information/events in chronological order. Present details in specific order to convey specific meaning.

When teachers show and explain these frames to Newcomers and place them on their Table Tents, they can begin to use one or two at a time with simple pieces of writing based on what they just read. Once the teacher models the stages of writing, they will be on their way to developing great writing skills.

In this approach, the teacher explicitly teaches and models prewriting, drafting, revising, editing, and publishing strategies (described in Figure 8.5); demonstrates and explains what the final written product should look like; provides exemplars for students to review; and explains and displays rubrics/criteria for assessment of that piece of writing. All the while, she addresses different stages of writing development and helps students with mini-lessons as necessary for each stage. Students should have opportunities to conference with and get feedback from peers and the teacher.

FIGURE 8.5 ExC-ELL's Writing Flow

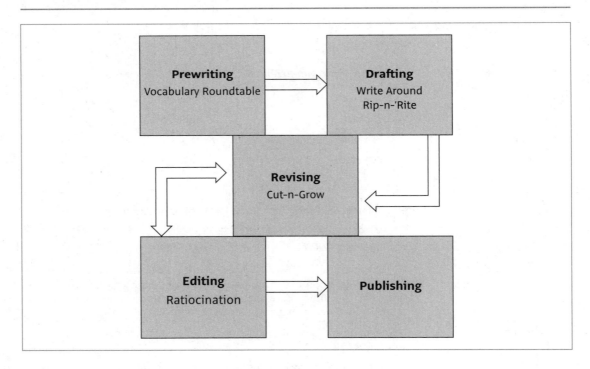

The Writing Stages

Writing is a recursive process, not a linear one, and needs to be taught explicitly and systematically in stages—drafting, editing, revising, and publishing.

Drafting

Writing in teams is the best way to start. Using the Write-Around strategy, every student gets involved. Write-Around is a team-based writing activity.

In this stage, students work in teams of three or four. As the teacher, you can give the following instructions, usually written on a SMART Board or shown on an overhead projector:

- Clear your desks.
- Each of you has one piece of paper and a pen or pencil.
- Each of you will copy the prompt and complete the sentence. The goal is to write about the topic of study and use related Tier 2 and Tier 3 words.
- After completing each sentence, you will pass the paper to the person to your right.
- The student receiving the paper will read what is written, add a sentence, and pass the paper to the right.
- Everyone will be writing at the same time. Each time you pass a paper to the right, your teammate will also be passing a paper to you.
- Read what your teammate wrote on the paper you just received and continue with the story.
- You will end up with several similar stories.
- The process will continue until I say "Stop!" (about 10 minutes).
- Do not write a conclusion now. We will write it later.

Students should fill about three-quarters of a page at minimum and write on only one side of the paper (the reason for which will become evident later). They need to write at least this much so that there is enough text to revise and edit.

In a Shelby County/Memphis middle school, we observed a Newcomer, on the first day of school and during the first period of the day, participate in the Write-Around. The teacher twinned the Newcomer with another EL who spoke Arabic, and they wrote together on all the papers.

Editing

Each student can use whichever piece of writing they are holding. There will be four similar papers, because each student continuously added a sentence to each of the papers as they circulated the table. They can choose one paper by reading aloud all four papers and choosing which one they would like to work on using a strategy called Ratiocination. Students focus on the rationale for using certain words over others or certain grammatical structures. This is a positive way of editing. No more red ink from the teacher! The teacher can conduct a brief lesson with 5 to 10 minutes of modeling and explaining to show how to self-correct a recurrent grammar or vocabulary problem. Students focus on only one area of corrections, one that the teacher has just taught about in the mini-lesson. Students can circle the words that need to be changed and then decide which ones to change. The teacher can select one area at a time from these examples to help students to see if they need to make that kind of correction:

- Students used too many repetitions of *the* or *they* at the beginning of each sentence, or *and, good, because* in other parts of the writing; students can replace these Tier 1 words with Tier 2 substitutions, such as *additionally, excellent,* or *due to*; they can replace *the* and *they* by naming the concept or proper noun.
- Students missed capital letters,
- There is subject-verb disagreement.
- Sentences are missing appropriate punctuation.
- Spelling needs to be fixed.

When working in a team, all students on the team need to review the one paper they have selected to share with the class later on. This means double, triple, or quadruple checking of the paper. Sometimes the writers ask the teacher to look at the paper before going on to the next phase. This is the easiest way for students to develop self-editing skills, improve their writing, and learn more language. After revising with the next phase, students can return to Ratiocination to do more editing.

Revising

For elaborating on sentences by adding more facts, evidence, or quotations and for constructing compound sentences or changing the sentence sequence, students can use the strategy we call Cut-n-Grow. Using this strategy also helps the teacher to explicitly teach when and how to add details and evidence to support the writer's claims. Here are steps for Cut-n-Grow; they can be done in a team of four, pairs, or individually:

1. Cut your team's composition right after the sentence where you as a team have agreed to add evidence/support for your claims or counterclaims (e.g., provide more facts).

2. On colored paper, write additional sentences and/or revised sentences.

3. Once finished, tape the rest of the composition on the colored sheet.

Publishing: Powerful Conclusion and Striking Title

Once the body of the composition is ready, the writer will add a powerful conclusion. There are different ways of ending a composition. You can create a student checklist addressing your district's requirements. The following are suggestions:

- Restate thesis statement.
- Summarize main points.
- Summarize evidence.
- End with a call to action, a question, a proposed solution, a thought-provoking quotation from the text, or a summary of what you learned.
- Use some of these transitions/connectors:
  —Given these points
  —As has been noted
  —All things considered
  —In the final analysis
  —As shown above
  —In summary
  —In closing

After the conclusion, add a striking title. Make the title something that will tell the reader what the piece is about and entice them into reading it.

Finally, it is time to read the final cut-up, rearranged, and pasted masterpiece, as refined by each team, to the whole class. It is displayed as is on a classroom wall or in the hall. In the Shelby schools, they are posted in the halls. They want everyone to see the process students have undertaken to compose a thoughtful, comprehensive piece that met the assignment criteria. Students are proud to present all the circled words and new words written above the changed word, all the added sentences where they cut and then grew on a different colored paper. The principal wants to see these messy masterpieces instead of the squeaky clean, typed white papers that almost always contain errors that have not been corrected.

From Prewriting to Publishing

The writing process, from the beginning, should be based on learned vocabulary and text-based content. Newcomers and other ELs benefit from team support. Beginning with Prewriting's Vocabulary Roundtable reviews, Newcomers, other ELs, and their colleagues realize and remember how much content-based vocabulary they have learned, plus collegial strategies to acquire and access more vocabulary from the Mentor Text.

Assessing Writing Instruction Processes Schoolwide

Returning with the final installment from Woodland Elementary, they focus on Writing Instruction. Remember, they were just starting to work on evaluating their program of instruction for ELs. If you haven't reviewed Woodland's Vocabulary Instruction assessment in Chapter 6 and Reading Comprehension and Instruction assessment in Chapter 7, now would be a good time to refresh your memory on where they were and the pieces that can help support writing acquisition. In Figure 8.6, we present an excerpt from what they came up with when they met to assess their students' writing skills and instruction needs after a team of teachers attended a state-sponsored ExC-ELL Institute. In their ExC-ELL PLC meeting, they returned to the rubric they had modified for the Vocabulary Instruction assessment and the Reading Comprehension and Instruction (Figures 6.5 and 7.5) and modified it again to create this rubric. In the "Started" column, they gave credit when it was due and used it as a base to begin assessing improvement. The team followed with the "Needed" column with notes on where the ExC-ELL TLC felt the improvement process should start. As with their rubrics in Figures 6.5 and 7.5, in the last column, named "Success," they worked on observable, measurable items that they would be able to use in their end-of-year report as evidence of improvement and implementation and as a base for moving forward for the following year.

In Figure 8.6, we provide a blank rubric. We provide the completed rubric in the Appendix. If you have read and worked through Chapters 6 and 7 before reading this chapter, then you should be familiar with how Woodland Elementary's rubric might look. Use the following write-up to complete the rubric. Then check your work in the Appendix.

FIGURE 8.6 Rubric for Writing Instruction and Assessment Strategies to Help ELs Succeed in Content Areas

Process/Component	Started (what we are doing now)	Needed (what else we need to do)	Success (evidence of improvement or implementation)
How do we preteach vocabulary as a base for the writing process?			
How do we use Mentor Texts as a base for the writing process?			
How do we infuse Text Structure into our writing instruction?			
What modeling and support do we provided for Newcomers/ELs for the writing process?			

continued

FIGURE 8.6 Rubric for Writing Instruction and Assessment Strategies to Help ELs Succeed in Content Areas (*continued*)

Process/ Component	Started (what we are doing now)	Needed (what else we need to do)	Success (evidence of improvement or implementation)
What writing process phases do we explicitly teach and use? What text/content-based writing strategies do we explicitly teach and use?			
What assessments and rubrics do we use for • Vocabulary? • Reading? • Writing? What data are we collecting?			
How many teachers do we still need to train in the recommended writing/assessment components from this chapter?			
Where are we on the Cycle of Instruction with our Newcomers and other ELs?			

Woodland Elementary Instruction for Newcomers and Other ELs: Overview, Next Steps, and EL Writing Instruction

At Woodland Elementary, we have used Writer's Workshop for the past 10 years. Some of our teachers have used it longer. In addition to the targeted vocabulary from our weekly vocabulary study lists, much of our curricula includes books to read as examples, additional writing activities, and pieces that had been added to our writing instruction. The ESL teacher, Mr. Quince, used the writing prompts and other types of activities provided in the district's ESL curriculum.

After attending the ExC-ELL Institute's Writing in the Content Area session, we reviewed our current instructional plans. For next year, we have added more specific instruction on modeling and using Tier 2 words and phrases. Our Language Objectives, assessment, and in-class usage expectations will be highlighted with each lesson, and we will debrief with the students to check for understanding. We will also use the Mentor Texts selected for lessons to highlight and model mechanics, features, structure, and grammar. Students will be expected to use evidence from the text to support claims or opinions in fiction and nonfiction texts.

The ExC-ELL TLC will continue to provide support and additional training to all teachers, focusing on mini-professional development sessions at grade level to support implementation of the Write-Around, Rip-n-'Rite, Ratiocination, and Cut-n-Grow strategies. Similarly, the ExC-ELL TLC will work with grade levels to develop rubrics and lessons that model expectations for writing in all content areas. Also included in the growth plan for next year will be a system for collecting daily performance assessment data to help show growth and inform instruction.

The Leadership Team, coaches, and teachers will be able to see evidence of implementation of these strategies during their Learning Walks and Peer Observations. While using the WISEcard, they will be able to note student work examples, evidence of deep dives into texts as sources for writing, and mastery of the content. Student writing samples posted on the walls will include team writings created with Write-Around, R.A.F.T., or Rip-n-'Rite. Editing and revising will be evidenced by student work samples that were Ratiocinated and improved via Cut-n-Grow. Ratiocination editing will include but will not be limited to Tier 2 and 3 sophisticated and specific vocabulary substituted for Tier 1 phrases, higher-order transitions and connectors, variations of sentence lengths, and corrected capitalization and punctuation. Appropriate Table Tents, posters, and other supports will be available to all students, with emphasis placed on ELs, Newcomers, and students with special educational needs.

Newcomers. Up until now, we have not had specific expectations of Newcomers for writing in the general classroom. Mr. Quince works with them during their ESL service hours using the district's curriculum. Beginning with the next school year, the Newcomer Teaching Team and Mr. Quince will develop rubrics for all teachers to use with the Newcomers in all domains, including writing, and will provide specific training for the entire staff, including the elective teachers, with a targeted goal of helping to reach our Newcomers and advance them through the curriculum.

Newcomers currently receive translated quizzes when possible. However, with the implementation of ExC-ELL strategies, students will be able to comprehend and practice the content they need to know to be able to participate in the same quizzes and assessments as their peers. They will have additional supports such as word banks, sentence starters, sentence frames, and shorter pieces from the grade-level text. Modifications will be provided as required by the LIEP or for any dually identified students with an IEP. In addition, informal data will serve as evidence of mastery and will be gathered on all students when participating in team writing activities such as Write-Around, R.A.F.T., and Rip-n-'Rite. We will also provide writing samples in each student's portfolio as evidence of mastery and usage.

Observers and the administration team will see Newcomers participating with their peers and growth at the end of the year on the WIDA ACCESS 2.0 tests and other end-of-year assessments.

Whole-School. Mr. Quince and the ExC-ELL-trained teachers have presented Write-Around, R.A.F.T., Rip-n-'Rite, Ratiocination, and Cut-n-Grow at a whole-staff meeting and grade-level meetings. They have invited and hosted teachers to watch these writing strategies in action. Moreover, they have volunteered to model these strategies in their classrooms. As noted, we will provide additional professional development sessions to revisit, adjust, and implement writing goals for each grade level's standards and curriculum. Ms. Puck and the Leadership Team, as noted in the Reading Comprehension report, have already planned a three-day ExC-ELL Institute for the beginning of next year and have emphasized that content-related, text-based writing skills will be a schoolwide expectation next year and that Woodland Elementary will be our pilot school for ExC-ELL. The ExC-ELL TLC facilitated this evaluation along with the vocabulary and reading comprehension evaluations and reports and will be working with the LIEP Committee to review this action plan for compliance.

Conclusion

Our process is not just about learning English quickly. If we slow our instructional process in the beginning, Newcomers and other ELs will be able to catch on quicker to all we want them to learn. As we described the processes for the 12 components, you probably thought, "But I don't have time to do all this! My pacing guide says I need to be on page x by next month." Hopefully now you see that this is doable and can be implemented with a little practice in any curriculum at any grade level and for any language.

We discovered a very significant premise from our longitudinal study on establishing and evaluating a two-way bilingual program in the El Paso Independent School District. Slow, deliberate reading of texts—taking time to learn vocabulary and discourse in two languages and to write from the beginning—accelerated Spanish and English speakers' language and academic standing. This was a 50-50 bilingual program. Fifty percent of the students were native English speakers, and 50 percent were native Spanish speakers (Newcomers and other ELs). Fifty percent of each day's instruction was in English and 50 percent in Spanish. English speakers helped Spanish-dominant students learn English. Spanish speakers helped English-dominant speakers learn Spanish. By the end of 5th grade, all were achieving at grade level. All were bilingual and biliterate. This was due to the fact that each year, their teachers took a couple of months to slow down the learning process, let students learn routines, language protocols, and how to read grade-level texts. By December or January, all students were ready to accelerate their learning in both languages. Hence, our recommendation is to slow down at the beginning to teach critical skills. Students will not only catch up but will accelerate their learning by spring-time testing.

As we experience an influx of Newcomers from multiple language groups and countries, we need to consider additional factors. When we immerse Newcomers in English classrooms without initial attention to acculturation to the U.S. educational system, we tend to turn them into LTELs. It is a moral injustice to these children, and it does nothing to improve our school accountability record. Therefore, we must seek a balance between socioemotional care and accelerated language, literacy, and content instruction. As we laid out in this text, all can be implemented simultaneously. There is no need to wait a whole year or a whole semester to help Newcomers adjust to their new environment. With finesse, love, and preparation from every teacher in the school, the balance can begin from day one of the Newcomers' arrival.

When it comes to accountability, our schools need to bring up with the school districts any efforts that seem to contradict current district policy. Districts reflect state policy. Yet, most state policies have not extensively explored all the possibilities ESSA now allows for EL schooling. Thus, it behooves us to anchor our efforts on ESSA using the rationale and effective instructional features that we have provided here. Due to the complexity of educating Newcomers, we can no longer leave it to a handful of amazing but rarely acknowledged ESL, ELD, and SEI teachers. It takes a whole school. With a whole-school effort, all students and adults succeed!

Appendix

Sample Completed Rubric for EL Services Evaluation & Analysis (Figure 4.2)

Adequate Number of Qualified EL Staff

Process/Component	Needed (planning notes)	Started (what else needed)	Successful (what we're looking for as proof)
Do all EL program, core-content, and special education teachers who instruct ELs have the appropriate certification, licensure, or training to teach ELs? If not, are they working to obtain it within a reasonable period of time?	Review all certifications.	Some teachers have attended EL strategy PD sessions but the whole school needs training.	All core-content, elective, and instructional support teachers have been trained in strategies to support EL learning in their content or area of specialization. PD hours or add-on certifications have been verified.
Do all teachers who instruct ELs demonstrate the skills necessary to effectively implement the EL program?	An observation protocol would help us gauge implementation all around and quality of instructional delivery.	Classroom Walk-Throughs and coaching sessions will be scheduled throughout the year. Expert coaches are also scheduled to visit classrooms to provide continued support and PD.	Evaluation, review, and analysis of the WISEcard observation protocols will provide a general report for an end-of-year evaluation and the planning of next steps for next year.

continued

Sample Completed Rubric for EL Services Evaluation & Analysis (Figure 4.2)

Adequate Number of Qualified EL Staff (*continued*)

Process/Component	Needed (planning notes)	Started (what else needed)	Successful (what we're looking for as proof)
Does the LEA or State Education Agency (SEA) provide supplemental professional learning opportunities, when necessary, to ensure that the EL program is implemented effectively?	Review PD offerings from the state and district. Evaluate need of teachers in our school.	Here in Virginia, our DOE provides multiple opportunities across the state each year, but more of our content teachers need to attend.	All state-provided PD session allotments should be filled, with certificates of participation verified.
Do all EL program, core-content, and special education teachers who deliver instruction to ELs with disabilities receive PD specifically related to teaching dually identified ELs?	No, this needs to be a part of the initial assessment and plan for our programs and teacher development.	The state DOE is providing a statewide PD session for dually identified ELs. Several teachers are signed up to attend.	PD hours or add-on certifications have been verified.
Are the LEA's EL services adequately staffed with qualified ESL, bilingual, core-content, and special education teachers trained in EL strategies, in order to meet ELs' language and content needs?	Our district sets these guidelines.	We have an ESL teacher shortage in our state. Some of our teachers are participating in state-funded endorsement programs.	We need additional teachers certified in ESL or validated as practitioners of ExC-ELL.
Are principals or other administrative staff tasked with evaluating EL teachers certified and sufficiently trained in EL strategies in order to meaningfully evaluate teachers who deliver instruction to ELs?	Our principals have been using the required evaluation forms. Now we need to find out how to use the WISEcard and how other school districts align both systems.	Our administration and leadership team will attend the ExC-ELL PD sessions with the teachers and the additional two-day ExC-ELL Admin Academy afterwards.	All administrators and leadership team members have attended and shown evidence of mastery via classroom Walk-Throughs and WISEcard-assisted observations.
Are paraprofessionals, staff, volunteers, or others adequately trained to support ELs, and are they working under the direct supervision of a qualified teacher?	We need to make sure they attend.	After attending the ExC-ELL Institute, several teachers have been tasked to redeliver these strategies to our other staff members.	Strategies are being implemented and faithfully used by all staff charged with helping students learn.

Sample Completed Rubric for Writing Instruction and Assessment Strategies
to Help ELs Succeed in Content Areas (Figure 8.6)

Process/Component	Started (what we are doing now)	Needed (what else do we need to do?)	Success (evidence of improvement or implementation)
How do we preteach vocabulary as a base for the writing process?	We use the vocabulary lists from our curriculum.	Implement more specific instructions on Tier 2 words and phrases. Model usage and inform students of expectations for usage.	Tier 2 words are posted in classrooms. Classroom instructional visits see teachers and students engaged in the 7 Steps. Vocabulary objectives show expected usage.
How do we use Mentor Texts as a base for the writing process?	We use the provided reading from our curricula for each subject.	Implement explicit instruction and expectations for: vocabulary usage mechanics, features, and structure use of evidence from the text to support claims or opinions.	Classroom instructional visits see teachers and students engaged in Think-Alouds, class debriefing on Mentor Texts, and written assignments that show connections to content-based texts.
How do we infuse text structure to into our writing instruction?	We give our students examples of different types of writing.	Implement more explicit instructions for and modeling of the target structure via Mentor Text examples.	Classroom instructional visits see teachers and students engaged in Think-Alouds. Written assignments show connections to targeted text structures. Students are provided with Table Tents and other supports.
What modeling and support do we provided for Newcomers/ELs for the writing process?	The ESL teacher works with these students.	Have all teachers learn how to help Newcomers and other ELs via the 5 Steps, Triad Reading, Triad Summarization, and team writing activities with supports.	Students are provided with and are using Table Tents. Newcomers are paired with partners for team writing activities.

continued

Process/ Component	Started (what we are doing now)	Needed (what else do we need to do?)	Success (evidence of improvement or implementation)
What writing process phases do we explicitly teach and use? What text/content-based writing strategies do we explicitly teach and use?	We do some prewriting, editing, and revising as scripted in our curricula according to subject. The ESL teacher works with the Newcomers to help with sentence construction and other mechanics.	Obtain specific training on (and implement) all phases as they relate to Newcomers and other ELs. Obtain training on team-based writing such as: • Write-Around • Rip-n-'Rite • Ratiocination • Cut-n-Grow	We use: • Table Tents • Wall charts/posters • Student writing samples • End-of-year data
What assessments and rubrics do we use for • Vocabulary? • Reading? • Writing? What data are we collecting?	We do not have specific rubrics for these components. We use test scores and grades.	Develop rubrics and model expectations for all learners. Collect daily informal data.	We use: • Completed rubrics • Student work samples • Table Tents
How many teachers do we still need to train in the recommended writing/assessment components from this chapter?	Our ESL teacher attended part of the training and has shared a few pieces.	Almost all teachers need training in how to support Newcomers and other ELs in these areas.	We have 100 percent completion of training and school action plan for continued support.
Where are we on the Cycle of Instruction with our Newcomers/ELs?	We are just starting.	Revisit our progress quarterly. Plan for annual review and refinement.	We have completed implementation and assessment rubrics with school action plan and program refinement plan.

Bibliography

August, D., Beck, I. L., Calderón, M. E., Francis, D. J., Lesaux, N. K., & Shanahan, T. (2008). Instruction and professional development. In D. August & T. Shanahan (Eds.), *Developing reading and writing in second-language learners. Lessons from the Report of the National Literacy Panel on Language-Minority Children and Youth.* New York: Routledge.

August, D., & Shanahan, T. (Eds.). (2008). *Developing reading and writing in second-language learners. Lessons from the Report of the National Literacy Panel on Language-Minority Children and Youth.* New York: Routledge.

Bandura, A. (1985). *Self-efficacy: The exercise of control.* New York: W. H. Freeman and Company.

Bear, D. R., Invernizzi, M., Templeton, S., & Johnston, F. (2016). *Words their way.* Upper Saddle River, NJ: Pearson.

Beck, I. L., McKeown, M. G., & Kucan, L. (2002). *Bringing words to life.* New York: Guilford.

Calderón, M. E. (1984). *Training bilingual trainers: An ethnographic study of coaching and its impact on the transfer of training.* (Doctoral dissertation.) In Dissertation Abstracts and Claremont Graduate School/San Diego State University.

Calderón, M. E. (2007). RIGOR! *Reading instructional goals for older readers: Reading program for 6th–12th students with interrupted formal education.* New York: Benchmark Education Co.

Calderón, M. E. (2011a). Teaching writing to English language learners. In *Teaching Writing to ELs in Secondary Schools*. Heslington, England: University of York.

Calderón, M. E. (2011b). *Teaching reading and comprehension to English learners, K–5*. Indianapolis, IN: Solution Tree.

Calderón, M. E. (2016). A whole-school approach to English learners. *Educational Leadership, 73*(5).

Calderón, M. E., Hertz-Lazarowitz, R., & Slavin, R. E. (Nov. 1998). Effects of bilingual cooperative integrated reading and composition on students making the transition from Spanish to English reading. *The Elementary School Journal, 99*(2). Retrieved from https://doi.org/10.1086/461920

Calderón, M. E., & Minaya-Rowe, L. (2011). *Preventing long-term English language learners: Transforming schools to meet core standards*. Thousand Oaks, CA: Corwin.

Calderón, M. E., & Slakk, S. (2018). *Expediting comprehension for English language learners (ExC-ELL) foundations manual* (3rd ed.). Washington, DC: Margarita Calderón & Associates.

Calderón, M. E., & Slakk, S. (2018). *Teaching reading to English learners, grades 6–12: A framework for improving achievement in the content areas* (2nd ed.). Thousand Oaks, CA: Corwin.

Calderón, M. E., Slakk, S., & Montenegro, H. (2017). *Promises fulfilled: A leader's guide for supporting English learners*. Bloomington, IN: Solution Tree.

Carroll, J. A., & Wilson, E. E. (2008). *Acts of teaching: How to teach writing* (2nd ed.). Portsmouth, NH: Heinemann.

Collaborative for Academic, Social, and Emotional Learning (CASEL). (2005). *Safe and sound: An educational leader's guide to evidence-based social and emotional learning (SEL) programs*. Chicago: Author.

Collaborative for Academic, Social, and Emotional Learning (CASEL). (2012). *Frequently asked questions about social and emotional learning (SEL)*. Chicago: Author.

Collaborative for Academic, Social, and Emotional Learning (CASEL). (2013). *CASEL school kit: A guide for implementing schoolwide academic, social, and emotional learning*. Chicago: Author.

Collaborative for Academic, Social, and Emotional Learning (CASEL). (2019). *What is SEL?* Retrieved from https://casel.org/what-is-sel/

Durlak, J. A., Weissberg, R. P., Dymnicki, A. B., Taylor, R. D., & Schellinger, K. B. (2011). The impact of enhancing students' social and emotional learning: A meta-analysis of school-based universal interventions. *Child Development, 82*(1), 405–432.

Elementary and Secondary Education Act (ESEA), 3113(b)(2) (2015). Retrieved from https://www2.ed.gov/policy/elsec/leg/esea02/pg41.html#sec3113

Geva, E., & Ramírez, G. (2015). *Focus on reading.* Oxford: Oxford University Press.

Goodwin, A. P., Huggins, A. C., Carlo, M. S., August, D., & Calderón, M. E. (2012). Minding morphology: How morphological awareness relates to reading for English language learners. *Reading and Writing, 26*(9). doi: 10.1007/s11145-012-9412-5

Graham, S., & Hebert, M. A. (2010). *Writing to read: Evidence for how writing can improve reading. A Carnegie Corporation Time to Act Report.* Washington, DC: Alliance for Excellent Education.

Hattie, J. A. C. (2015). *What doesn't work in education: The politics of distraction.* London: Pearson.

Igoa, C. (1995). *The inner world of the immigrant child.* New York: St. Martin's Press.

Lee, C. D., & Spratley, A. (2010). *Reading in the disciplines: The challenges of adolescent literacy.* New York: Carnegie Corporation of New York.

LeMoine, N., & Soto, I. (2017). *Academic language mastery: Culture in context.* Thousand Oaks, CA: Corwin.

Migration Policy Institute. (2016). *Health and social service needs of U.S.-citizen children with detained or deported immigrant parents.* Retrieved from https://www.migration policy.org/research/health-and-social-service-needs-us-citizen-children-detained-or-deported-immigrant-parents

National Academies of Sciences, Engineering, and Medicine. (2017). *Promoting the educational success of children and youth learning English: Promising futures.* Washington, DC: The National Academies Press. doi: 10.17226/24677

Showers, B., & Joyce, B. (2002). *Student achievement through staff development* (3rd ed.). Alexandria, VA: ASCD.

Slavin, R. E., Madden, N. A., Calderón, M. E., Chamberlain, A., & Hennessy, M. (2011). Reading and language outcomes of a five-year randomized evaluation of transitional bilingual education. *Educational Evaluation and Policy Analysis, 33*(1), 47–58. Retrieved from http://www.edweek.org/media/bilingual_pdf.pdf

Soto-Hinman, I., & Hetzel, J. (2009). *The literacy gaps: Building bridges for ELLs and SELs.* Thousand Oaks, CA: Corwin.

U.S. Department of Education. (2007). *What works clearinghouse.* Retrieved from https://ies.ed.gov/ncee/wwc/

U.S. Department of Education. (2015). *English learner tool kit for state and local education agencies (SEAs and LEAs)*. Retrieved from https://ncela.ed.gov/files/english_learner_toolkit/OELA_2017_ELsToolkit_508C.pdf

U.S. Department of Education. (2015). *Newcomer tool kit*. Retrieved from www2.ed.gov/about/offices/list/oela/newcomers-toolkit/ncomertoolkit.pdf

U.S. Department of Education. (November 2016). *Tools and resources for providing ELs with a language assistance program*. Retrieved from http://www2.ed.gov/about/offices/list/ocr/ellresources.html

U.S. Department of Justice & U.S. Department of Education. (January 7, 2015). *Dear colleague letter: English learner students and limited English proficient parents*. Washington, DC: U.S. Department of Justice Civil Rights Division & U.S. Department of Education Office for Civil Rights. Retrieved from https://www.justice.gov/sites/default/files/crt/legacy/2015/01/07/eldcleng.pdf

Watts-Taffe, S., & Truscott, D. (2000). Using what we know about language and literacy for ESL students in the mainstream classroom. *Language Arts, 77*(3), 258–265.

Zins, J. E., Weissberg, R. P., Wang, M. C., & Walberg, H. J. (Eds.). (2004). *Building academic success on social and emotional learning: What does the research say?* New York: Teachers College Press.

Index

Note: The letter *f* following a page number denotes a figure.

About the Authors

 **Margarita Espino Calderón, PhD**, Professor Emerita, Johns Hopkins University, has served on national preschool to 12th grade literacy panels and as an advisory board member of the National Research Council, the Education Testing Service, WIDA, the National Center for Learning Disabilities, the National Literacy Panel for Language-Minority Children and Youth, and the Carnegie Adolescent English Language Learners Literacy Panel. She is a consultant for the U.S. Department of Justice and the Office of Civil Rights. Her research interests include professional development, effective schools, and language and literacy development of English learners.

Dr. Calderón served as principal investigator of ExC-ELL—Expediting Comprehension for English Language Learners—a five-year study of middle and high schools funded by the Carnegie Corporation of New York and, with Robert Slavin, as co-principal investigator of both a five-year randomized evaluation of English immersion, transitional, and two-way bilingual elementary programs and BCIRC—Bilingual Cooperative Integrated Reading and Composition—a five-year study of elementary schools, both funded by the Institute for Education Sciences and the United States Department of Education.

Dr. Calderón, a former middle and high school teacher, directed bilingual professional development programs at San Diego State University and taught bilingual and educational leadership courses at the University of Texas, El Paso and University of California, Santa Barbara. She has authored, coauthored, or edited more than 100 books, articles, and chapters, is an international speaker, and conducts comprehensive professional development programs throughout the United States and abroad.

Shawn Slakk is vice president of operations and senior consultant, Margarita Calderón & Associates, where he and his colleagues train teachers and administrators how to consolidate language, literacy, and content for English learners and all other students. Shawn is coauthor and developer of professional development sessions focusing on whole-school implementation, administrative support, and coaching. He serves as the lead ExC-ELL consultant for the state of Virginia. Recent projects include redesigning ExC-ELL for adult learners, implemented at the Ana G. Mendez University System campuses in Washington, DC, Florida, and Dallas, Texas.

Slakk who taught elementary and middle school ESL and Spanish and served as a school administrator, is the former coordinator of RETELL—Rethinking Equity and Teaching for English Language Learners—for the Massachusetts Department of Elementary and Secondary Education, where he and his staff developed the Sheltered English Instruction endorsement courses for administrators and classroom teachers.

As a former certified WIDA trainer and coach for the Sheltered Instruction Observation Protocol, Slakk provided professional development on instructional strategies, lesson delivery, and assessment to support ELs. He earned a bachelor's degree in K–12 English Education and K–12 Spanish Education from Whitworth College and master's degrees in Teaching English to Speakers of Other Languages—TESOL—from Eastern Washington University and in school administration from the University of North Carolina Greensboro. He is currently pursuing a doctorate degree in curriculum and instruction with an emphasis on reading and writing instruction for additional language learners at the University of Virginia.

Related ASCD Resources: English Language Learners

At the time of publication, the following resources were available (ASCD stock numbers appear in parentheses):

Print Products

Fostering Resilient Learners: Strategies for Creating a Trauma-Sensitive Classroom by Kristin Souers with Pete Hall (#116014)

Turning High-Poverty Schools into High-Performing Schools by William H. Parrett and Kathleen M. Budge (#109003)

Reaching Out to Latino Families of English Language Learners by David Campos, Rocio Delgado, and Mary Esther Soto Huerta (#110005)

Teaching English Language Learners Across the Content Areas by Judie Haynes and Debbie Zacarian (#109032)

The Language-Rich Classroom: A Research-Based Framework for Teaching English Language Learners by Pérsida Himmele and William Himmele (#108037)

Managing Diverse Classrooms: How to Build on Students' Cultural Strengths by Carrie Rothstein-Fisch and Elise Trumbull (#107014)

Content-Area Conversations: How to Plan Discussion-Based Lessons for Diverse Language Learners by Douglas Fisher, Nancy Frey, and Carol Rothenberg (#108035)

Educating Everybody's Children: Diverse Teaching Strategies for Diverse Learners, Revised and Expanded 2nd Edition by Robert W. Cole (#107003)

Getting Started with English Language Learners: How Educators Can Meet the Challenge by Judie Haynes (#106048)

Research-Based Methods of Reading Instruction for English Language Learners, Grades K–4 by Sylvia Linan-Thompson and Sharon Vaughn (#108002)

Leading an Inclusive School: Access and Success for ALL Students by Richard A. Villa and Jacqueline S. Thousand (#116022)

For up-to-date information about ASCD resources, go to www.ascd.org. You can search the complete archives of *Educational Leadership* at www.ascd.org/el.

ASCD myTeachSource®

Download resources from a professional learning platform with hundreds of research-based best practices and tools for your classroom at http://myteachsource.ascd.org/.

For more information, send an e-mail to member@ascd.org; call 1-800-933-2723 or 703-578-9600; send a fax to 703-575-5400; or write to Information Services, ASCD, 1703 N. Beauregard St., Alexandria, VA 22311-1714 USA.

WHOLE CHILD TENETS

WHOLE CHILD
TENETS

1 HEALTHY
Each student enters school healthy and learns about and practices a healthy lifestyle.

2 SAFE
Each student learns in an environment that is physically and emotionally safe for students and adults.

3 ENGAGED
Each student is actively engaged in learning and is connected to the school and broader community.

4 SUPPORTED
Each student has access to personalized learning and is supported by qualified, caring adults.

5 CHALLENGED
Each student is challenged academically and prepared for success in college or further study and for employment and participation in a global environment.

The ASCD Whole Child approach is an effort to transition from a focus on narrowly defined academic achievement to one that promotes the long-term development and success of all children. Through this approach, ASCD supports educators, families, community members, and policymakers as they move from a vision about educating the whole child to sustainable, collaborative actions.

Success with Multicultural Newcomers & English Learners relates to the **healthy**, **engaged**, **supported**, and **challenged** tenets.

For more about the ASCD Whole Child approach, visit **www.ascd.org/wholechild.**